The Village London Atlas

THE GROWTH OF VICTORIAN
LONDON 1822–1903

The Village London Atlas

THE GROWTH OF VICTORIAN
LONDON 1822–1903

The Village Press

Published by The Village Press Limited
7d Keats Parade, Church Street, Edmonton, N9 9DP.

September 1989.

Originally published in hardback
by The Alderman Press in November 1986
Reprinted January 1987, September 1988
and June 1989

British Library Cataloguing in Publication Data

The Village London atlas: the changing face of Greater London 1822-1903

    1. London (England) _____ Maps
    912'.412   G1819.L7

ISBN: 0-946619-26-3
ISBN: 1 85540 015 4 pbk.

Typesetting by Stone Associates, Winchmore Hill.
Printed and Bound in Gt Britain by
Staples Printers (Rochester) Limited,
Love Lane, Rochester, Kent.

Acknowledgements.

The publishers would like to thank the following for their great help during the preparation
of this Atlas.

The staff of the Map Library and Photographic Department of The British Library.

Graham Dalling. Archivist for the London Borough of Enfield.

All maps reproduced by kind permission of The British Library.

Chapter I
A Victorian's view of changing London.
by
Percy Fitzgerald

One only has to read a few lines of Percy Fitzgerald's book – 'Victoria's London – The Suburbs' – to realise what a tremendous feeling, as well as knowledge, he had for old London. There was at that time, the 1880's and 1890's, a great welling up of nostalgia for London's past which equals that of today. Perhaps it is the almost unconcious feeling that the century is drawing to a close which brings this about, certainly there is parallel with our own time. At any rate when an introductory chapter was required for The Village London Atlas we needed to look no further than the opening chapter of Victoria's London.

The Publishers.

For the true Londoner nothing can be so pleasing as to note the affectionate interest that is now shown in the history of his much-loved city. Within a few years there has been a general revival of interest in this fascinating subject. Artists and writers have explored unfrequented quarters and forgotten lanes, in search of all that is picturesque; thus lending attraction to the magazine or to some imposing tome, such as was the predecessor of the present. It would seem as if these ardent labourers were hurrying to be in time to secure some record at least of the older monuments; indeed, it is now necessary to use all convenient speed; for every day and hour almost is bringing with it its note of coming destruction, and the paragraph "Disappearing London" recurs with alarming frequency. Every old house or old church or college may be said to be under sentence; for it "cumbereth" valuable ground. It is almost pathetic to note the fine old house in the suburbs standing in its fair gardens and lawns looking on the highroad; for it is already marked by the spoiler. Some forty or fifty years hence this rapacious greed will have wrought incalculable havoc. Business men and practical-minded persons seem to have a positive dislike to any old memorials of the kind. They would have them carted away: among the symmetrical modern structures they seem an eyesore. Soon or late, and more likely soon, there is certain to be a combined onslaught on the City churches, whose sites are coveted for palatial City warehouses, and such pressure it will be difficult to resist. When a substantial morsel of the old Roman wall is laid open to view in digging foundations, the utmost grace accorded is a day or two's delay to allow the antiquaries to come and see it.

One of the most interesting things in the study of London is the variety, the marked distinction, between the component parts that make up the great whole. We are told of the "growth of London," of the yearly absorption of outlying districts; but London has never become one homogeneous mass. Yet, in spite of all, it still remains "London City," with London Suburbs attached to it; and a continued familiarity prevents us observing how all these annexed districts retain marked characteristics of their own. A stranger taken for the first time through the various quarters could hardly fail to note their distinctive character. Thus Westminster, "Belgravia," Mayfair, Islington, Knightsbridge, St. John's Wood, the Regent's Park, The Boltons, the new Queen Anne district ("Cadogan Land," as we might style it) the "Borough", Paddington, Pimlico, and many more such quarters, all offer "notes" and peculiarities of their own. The more "official" suburbs, such as Chelsea and Kensington, or St. John's Wood, still retain, in spite of the efforts of the builder, a kind of rural air: in Buckingham Palace Road, close to Victoria Station, there is still to be seen the survival of gardens in front of the houses; while in a street within view of Sloane Square only a year or two ago were to be found the green roadside wooden palings, stunted trees, with public-house signs suspended from posts. This individuality has been not a little fostered by the erection of Town Halls, which suggest an idea of municipal independence, and which tend to concentrate all the local

energies. A concert—say at the Westminster Town
Hall—has quite an air of local festivity; we seem to be in
a provincial town where some rare gala has roused the
natives into some excitement. A walk through the High
Street of Southwark or Bishopsgate Street suggests a
prosperous country town. There is a snug, old-fashioned
air, with framed and gabled houses here and there hedged
in between more pretentious neighbours; while the shops
have a provincial glitter. The waggons and carriers' carts
are moving slowly out countrywards. The ponderous
church has a rural look. Or, as we pass out of Harley Street
into the Marylebone Road, what an abrupt change!
We are in a suburb at once: here are villas walled round,
such as Dickens's house, presenting large gardens, and a
sort of "high-road," with trees, and other rural
accompaniments. With this we may contrast the little
"shabby-genteel" streets of Mayfair, which have their
psychological meaning; for a poor district promoted into
fashion signifies houses on valuable sites. Dickens and
Thackeray, who understood their London psychology
well, have interpreted these odd concatenations. And who
will say that there is not a distinct physiognomy in the
dreary, chilling lines of Wimpole Street, Harley Street,
and their neighbours, where the houses have, as it were,
been "run" in the one mould? There seems some fitness
in the one perpetual succession of gloomy doctors'
parlours and patients' rooms, where sentences of life
and death are being waited for all the day long. So with
the region of the great squares – Grosvenor, Berkeley,
and Portman – there is a tone of solid, old-fashioned state,
and every second house seems a mansion. How curious
too are the feelings aroused by the Bayswater region!
Here we find wastes of "compo" mansions, terraces and
squares in abundance, and trees also. There is a general
pretentiousness—from the uniform, stuccoed balustrades,
the languid trees, and dusty foliage. "Middle-class" folk
live in these would-be palaces and terraces. Mixed up
invariably with this affected state, we find streets, rows of
flashy shops, and all the vulgar incidents of traffic,
omnibuses, carts, etc. Then, turning to "Queen Anne's
land" by Knightsbridge, we seem to find ourselves
transported to some Dutch city: every house ruby red, each
competing with its neighbour in fantastic shapes and
outlines. Or we take a flight to Westminster, to that street
of monstrous, beetling houses,—Victoria Street,—all
chambers and offices and hotels signifying but a temporary
occupation and a flitting to the country or suburbs
when the day's work is done. Or we may hurry to the
modern district of South Kensington, with its palatial
mansions, somewhat out of fashion and deserted, but
which sprang up at a season of "inflation", when every
one was, or fancied he was, growing rich. Now it is found
that small but roomy houses are "your only wear." Or
we may flit to that forlorn district beyond Islington
where there are rows upon rows of yellow villas, stuccoed,
well smirched, stained, and decayed, and with a spurious
air of country—villas that had seen better days, but

now inexpressibly forlorn and decayed, patched and
stained.

It adds a piquancy to our London promenades to note
the many survivals of the old suburban character,
which are to be encountered in even the most urban
districts. Habit soon helps to detect readily these
marks and tokens. The familiar Primrose Hill, that
breezy playground, is now encompassed by streets and
houses, though it commands a pleasant view of the
northern heights. It is difficult to realise that in this
very public place, once so secluded and free from
interruptions, what was the last duel in England was
fought, on a post then known as Chalk Farm. Again,
in the rather rustic-looking street Davies Street, close
to Berkeley Square, we may note a gloomy, well-
grimed mansion, set at an angle to the street, with a
court or scrap of garden in front, Bourdon House, as
it is called; it was once a part of the Old Manor House,
a country seat of the opulent Davies, the lord of the
soil. It therefore once stood on the country road; and
here are Farm Street and Hill Street close by. The
Jesuit church has for forty years and more stood in
what is literally a stable lane, or mews, rudely paved.

A quaintly-minded Londoner seeking to appreciate
better his loved city once conceived the idea, old
established resident as he was, of *travelling* through
London, and of sojourning in the different quarters so
as to participate in their tone and flavour. With this
view he first put up at the vast foreign-looking hotel
on the Embankment, from whose window as he rose
in the morning he could see the whole river life: the
barges moving languidly by, the flitting steamers.
Thence he moved on to the huge Midland Hotel at St.
Pancras, a little city in itself, full of animation and life,
situated high in the air, in a sort of Islington bustle; and
whence he saw London, through the eyes, as it were, of
innumerable northerners who had come to town. What
a bustle from converging tram lines! what a fine air,
and splendid views of the heights of Hampstead and
Highgate and the country generally! hence he passed
to the Great Western Hotel at Paddington, where he
found a world of another complexion; the tame yellow
houses of Westbourne and other terraces being close
by, with a curious general stagnation: these side by
side with a "huckstering" neighbourhood, streets and
shops of a poorish sort. Later he sat him down at one
of the curious hostelries in Charterhouse Square, where
he seemed to be in an ancient country town, or in
one of those inns of fiction where say Mr. Squeers might
have alighted. There were other houses of which he made
trial, such as the Arundel, the resort of country sight-seers,
and where he lived, as it were, close to the roar of the
Strand. He may have found the most original experience
of all at the Covent Garden Hotel, situated in the market,
and finally at the great "Metropole" hard by Trafalgar
Square. No one who had not enjoyed these experiences,
he protested, could have any idea of what the great

city really was. Yet the unobservant resident who has known his London for a life will take little note of these dramatic differences.

The growth and absorption of territory has been as sudden as it is rapid. There is many an "old inhabitant" whose father must have "minded the time" when London was a huge detached city, the country coming up to its gates; it is only within average living memory that almost every rural outlet has been closed up by buildings. Towards the end of last century the Duke of Bedford's great mansion, which filled the northern side of Bloomsbury Square, had a clear uninterrupted view of Hampstead and Highgate. The open country too came up close by Portland Road and all the district round. "The Foundling" hard by, when built lay really in the country. It is more astonishing to think that there must be people now alive who recall the time when the Regent's Park was a waste of pasture land, and its terraces were not.

A significant proof of the gradual absorption by London City of all adjoining suburbs is found in the number of "High Streets" which we find in all quarters of the city: such for instance as High Street, Marylebone. This was, of course, the main and chief street in each suburb. There are, indeed, over a score of streets so named. But, as has been often said, a sort of history of London could be roughly evolved from the very names of its streets.

An idea of how tremendous is this ever-growing, ever-absorbing London may be conceived from some figures which are of a startling kind. It contains some five millions of inhabitants, increased every year by over fifty thousand souls. The value of its houses, property, etc., is rated at some thirty millions of pounds annually, and its trade, import and export, at two hundred millions. Nearly seven hundred thousand houses and buildings are spread over some seven hundred square miles, and there are—and this is truly astonishing—three thousand miles of streets. Four millions of sheep and nine millions of poultry and game are consumed in the year!

A casual glance at the map issued "'tis sixty years since" — not a very great stretch backwards — shows us how this great London has expanded with leaps and bounds, as it were. Then, Brompton, Chelsea, Pimlico, and Knightsbridge, were comparatively uncovered by streets; Kennington, Vauxhall, and Southwark, were open to Deptford. Poplar or the Isle of Dogs, was a comparative blank; so were Bethnal Green, Hackney, Islington, Camden and Kentish Towns. Islington, Pentonville, Hackney, Bethnal Green, were each crossed by a road or street, while Paddington and Bayswater offered stretches of territory with but few houses and fewer streets.

London City, like British rule in India, has drawn all. But it is the southern side of the river that offers the most extraordinary contrast to what it presents in our time. In 1833 the only portion that was laid out in streets and houses and might be considered "town"

was the portion comprised within the curve of the river, and bounded by a line drawn from Lambeth Palace by Newington, and ending at Bermondsey. Outside this "pale," as we might call it, all lay open. Beginning where Battersea Park now is, we find a great waste, formerly known as Battersea Fields, where "the Duke" fought a political duel without being interrupted, and whither he rode out as to the country. We pass by "Nine Elms," leaving the Vauxhall gardens on our left. Between the gardens and Lambeth Palace was an open tract, which spread away to Newington Butts and Kennnington, whose "common" was then unenclosed. Another tract, comprising Walworth and Rotherhithe, led on to Deptford and Greenwich, It is extraordinary to contrast with this the densely populated streets that in a short space of time have since spread over these regions. Again, the abolition or destruction of Brompton, its fair grounds, villas, and market gardens, with the creation of the new Kensingtons, dates only from the Exhibition year, 1851. To the Crystal Palace we owe the creation of the great Norwood and Sydenham districts; while "Belgravia," with its streets and fine squares, was laid out within living memory, as well as the newer and less aristocratic district that stretches from Buckingham Palace Road down to the river. Russell Square, once sacred to lawyers, was laid out so recently as 1804, which shows how rapid has been the growth of the great city. The picturesque little Queen Square in Bloomsbury, which has its side to the north uncovered by houses, testifies significantly to this vicinity of the country; for the space was purposely left vacant so that, as an old writer says, the denizens of the square might command a full view of the "beautiful landscape" and the northern heights. And Mr. Wheatley tells us that in certain streets of this district the northern side is a story or two lower, so as not to interrupt their opposite neighbour's view.

We could imagine nothing more interesting than a series of these comparative maps on the same scale, showing the gradual increase of London territory. One of only thirty or forty years ago set beside one of the present day would excite almost as much astonishment as the old one of Aggas put beside a great railway map of to-day. One of the best topographical pictures of London suburbs over one hundred years ago is Dodsley's account, which is welcome for its natural, unaffected style, and the tone of admiring awe with which the wonders of the town are depicted.

Were we to impress a stranger with an idea of the grandeur and splendour of this London of ours, we should lead him—not to the heart of the City, or to the Bank, Charing Cross, Fleet Street, or to Rotten Row, or to the "Church Parade" in Hyde Park of a Sunday morning — we should place him at the middle of Westminster Bridge with his face to St. Paul's. There we would see the long line of gigantic buildings stretching away on the left like palaces; the new red police office; the Whitehall Terrace, with Somerset House beyond; the huge hotels; the great

Embankment below, with its richly verdant belt of plane trees; the light and not unpleasing railway bridge; the noble Waterloo Bridge, worthy of old Rome; the other bridges beyond; St.Paul's and the City spires in the distance; while below are the ever-flitting steamboats, the barges, following the majestic bends of the great river. Then we turn and see just behind us the luxuriantly Gothic pile of the Houses of Parliament, with the terraces and pinnacles; the scattered, cheerful-looking buildings of the great hospital on the other side of the river; while to our right are the converging streets at Palace Yard, – one of the busiest quarters of London, – with the fine Clock Tower, and a glimpse of the Park beyond. All this combination suggests an idea of power, traffic, and magnificence that no other city can furnish. This dramatic scene is likely to escape many who are too engrossed to pause on their way, and who hurry across the bridge in pursuit of their business. And all has been but the growth of the last twenty or thirty years. It is curious to contrast with this bustling picture the reflections of the great poet who stood on the older bridge years ago, and expressed his feelings in a famous sonnet:

Earth hath not anything to show more fair.
The city now doth like a garment wear
The beauty of the morning: silent, bare,
Ships, towers, domes, theatres, and temples lie
Open unto the fields, and to the sky;
All bright and glittering in the smokeless air.

A tranquil, almost rural scene. At that time—well-nigh a century ago—the busiest portion of the river was beyond London Bridge, where, in the once proverbial phrase, "the forest of masts" was to be seen. "Forest of funnels" is now more appropriate; the masts have retreated to the innumerable docks. Wordsworth then saw but a sedgy foreshore, lined with shanties, sheds, and small warehouses: there too stood Inigo Jones's Water Gate at the edge of the water, washed by the stream; and the terrace or "mall" which then touched the river. No suspension or railway bridge was at Hungerford Stairs. The Adelphi Terrace, then new and conspicuous, was admired as a sort of monumental structure, and there was no fringe of vast buildings between the river and the shadowy outlines of St. Paul's.

Percy Fitzgerald, c.1890

Chapter II
A brief outline of the pattern of change in Victorian London
by
B.R. Bruff

On today's maps, London appears as an unbroken sprawl of bricks and mortar from Enfield in the north to Purley in the south, from Uxbridge in the West to Hornchurch and Upminster in the east. Yet only a century-and-a-half ago, the city's limits extended barely beyond Shoreditch and Westminster, Finsbury and Southwark. Outside these limits was a landscape of farmland, heath, wood and marsh, hamlets, villages and small market towns. Today's inner city areas, Hackney for example, were pleasant semi-rural suburbs, populated by wealthy city gentry.

The rapidity of London's expansion is remarkable. Between 1816 and 1880 the city spread outwards, with the two main booms in building occurring between 1816 and 1826 and 1868 and 1880; a third took place in the first decade of the present century. When they were over, the rural hinterland had ceased to exist, and London had taken on more or less its modern shape.

The first areas to be affected by the sudden growth of London were Paddington and Bayswater, Stoke Newington, Hackney, Clapham and Camberwell, but like a creeping tide development moved on and village after village found itself part of the 'Great Wen' and the 'cockney' had to go farther afield for his day in the country.

To Victorian historians like Edward Walford, Walter Thornbury and Percy Fitzgerald, it seemed that the London that they knew and loved so well was disappearing before their eyes, and they made it their mission in life to describe it for future generations before it vanished entirely. Londoners owe them a debt of gratitude.

Thornbury and Walford, particularly in their momumental works, London Recollected and Village London, recorded every old street and building inn and palace. Village and hamlet, manor and farm, all were described. Every person of note, whether they were prince or peasant has their own niche in this history. They wrote against a backcloth of tremendous change; social, political, financial, and, while they railed against the disappearance of the lovely countryside that lay around London, they knew nothing was going to stop it.

Fitzgerald, writing in the 1890's, says of villages like Greenford, Wembley and Dollis Hill: 'These places can scarcely be considered within the range of 'suburban London'. But they are clearly marked down for absorption as much as Hampstead and Norwood were. The process is prompt and speedy. One day the fair smiling place is found out and speedily covered with terraces and buildings, and from that moment it begins to stretch its hand to the Metropolis, eager to join it'.

And so it proved. The Capital's ever-increasing population created an insatiable demand for new housing. In the century between 1811 and 1911, the population of the County of London as a whole quadrupled, rising from 1,139,355 to 4,521,685, and in some areas the increase was almost two hundred-fold: Hampstead, for example, saw the number of its inhabitants grow from 3,483 to 85,945 (Census of England and Wales.)

When one drives across London today, it is next to impossible to imagine the landscape of wooded hills and winding narrow lanes that existed a bare century ago. By change — or, in some fortunate cases, foresight—vestiges remain: Epping Forest, Hampstead Heath and Wimbledon Common are major examples, Highgate Woods another. The hawthorns that line the North Circular Road at Finchley are the last remnants of Finchley Common, where once highwaymen like Dick Turpin lay in wait for coaches climbing up out of London, and where, in 1724, Jack Shephard was finally captured after his escape from Newgate Prison. For many years the northern boundary of London was the great New Road, the city's first bypass. Begun in

1836, it eventually become the Marylebone Road, Euston Road and Pentonville Road of today. Beyond, from the flat fields of Greenford round to the Northern Heights of Hampstead and Highgate was farmland, devoted mostly to the production of hay for the thousands of horses working in London, and worked by gangs of men moving from field to field and farm to farm in rotation. But during the early 1800's, like floodwaters released from behind a bursting dam, the tide of houses surged northwards.

Much of the initial development took place along the line of the turnpike roads which radiated out from the city to the rim of the London Basin, where towns like Romford, Barnet, Epping, Watford, Uxbridge, Kingston, Croydon and Dartford stand. These turnpikes were for the most part based on the network of Roman Roads – Watling Street, for example, the modern Edgware Road, leading to Chester, and Ermine Street, running through Shoreditch, Dalston, Stamford Hill and Tottenham on its way to Lincoln. Between these arterial roads meandered the old medieval field ways.

The turnpike roads were built for the swifter and smoother progress of the stage coaches, which for some two centuries provided the sole means of long-distance passenger transport. At the height of the coaching age, over 150 a day passed through High Barnet (known then as Chipping Barnet) on the Great North Road alone. There they would mingle with the great herds of livestock being driven southwards to feed London's growing population. To the people of those days, modern traffic would probably seem calm and orderly in comparison.

As road surfaces improved and commuting into London became easier, ribbon development took place along the line of the turnpikes. Comfortable suburbs such as Clapham, Hampstead, Hackney, St. John's Wood grew up as the middle classes took their new wealth out of the overcrowded city. The Georgian houses that front Camden Road, Clapton Road, Mildmay Park and other areas which have escaped Hitler's bombers and modern-day property developers bear witness to this early expansion. Very probably to the consternation of their owners, industry too moved out of the city, and workers' dwellings rapidly filled in the spaces between the mansions.

The real acceleration of London's outward growth began with the coming of the railways in the 1830's, which sounded the death knell of both the turnpike roads and the stagecoaches. Today one can see at Seven Sisters the result of this, for here the Eastern Counties Turnpike, begun in the 1820's to provide a most necessary good road between London and East Anglia, was abandoned in 1834. Those generations of travellers who have since arrived at Manor House to face a crawl through the narrow streets of Harringay, Tottenham, Edmonton and Clapton now know who to blame.

Nevertheless, it was to be some years before the railway companies realised the profit that might be made from commuter traffic and began to open suburban stations – their principal objective was to reach London from the provinces. Once the local stations began to open, though, the days of rural London were numbered. Wood Green, for instance, described by Walford as 'a retired country spot, hemmed in by green lanes and sturdy hedgegrows, where the ruralising cockney might betake himself in the summertime'. The building of Alexandra Palace Station by the Great Northern Railway soon changed all that; in the space of twenty years Wood Green was a thriving industrial area and 'ruralising' only a distant memory. North and East London along the lines of the Great Northern and Great Eastern Railways were, indeed, among the first areas to feel the effects, Stamford Hill, Tottenham and Edmonton soon joining hands, and Bromley, Bow, West Ham, Stratford and Ilford doing likewise. Wherever a station was opened, the speculators moved in, buying up the large houses, the farms and the nurseries and erecting row upon row of workmen's cottages, doubtless to the chagrin of the local gentry, and doubtless to their profit also.

Certainly the aristocrats who owned by far the major proportion of the land in and around London – the Dukes of Portland and Bedford, Marquis Camden, Lord Southampton and others whose names are commemorated in the districts they once owned – substantially increased their fortunes by the sale of their lands, though they allowed the railways to have as little effect as possible on their estates, driving them underground and into culverts wherever they could. Elsewhere, with powers given by Parliament, the railway companies drove in roughshod, displacing thousands of people in the process, with no obligation, it seems, to rehouse them. In inner London, where vast areas were needed for the great termini, for sidings and junctions, engine sheds and repair depots, hundreds of houses were demolished. One whole area, Agar Town, was erased from the map entirely. The railways built imposing hotels, many still to be seen, though very few now serve their original purpose, and shopping parades followed soon after.

In East London, the population of Stratford, Canning Town, Barking, Leyton, Leytonstone, Walthamstow, Wanstead and Woodford, doubled from 112,000 to 224,000 in the decade between 1871 and 1881. Many of the new inhabitants of these districts were forced to move into them from the City because of the loss of their homes to railway and road-building. In East Ham and West Ham, where the land had previously been used for market gardening, there was a similar rise. The greatest increase in this area was around Plaistow, which by 1881 had grown from a small village, lacking even a church, to an industrial suburb with a population of 67,000. This spectacular growth was due to the effect of the railways and the Victoria

Dock, later to become the Victoria and Albert Docks. These alone employed some 12,000 men. New industries were springing up in the area now called Silvertown, named for Mr. Silver's India-Rubber Clothing Factory.

The West London areas of Hammersmith, Kensington, Fulham, Acton and Chiswick were all swallowed up. In 1861 Willesden had a population of less than 4,000; in ten years this had quadrupled, and by 1881 almost doubled again. Willesden Green, once one of the most rustic spots near London, with its 'Spotted Dog' tavern and tea-garden, was covered with homes in a generation. Here, the railway had almost as much impact as at Clapham, with five lines meeting at Willesden Junction, and huge new yards being built. With the stations at Brondesbury, Kensal Green, Harrow Road and Neasden a completely new district developed, Stonebridge Park, where previously had stood a handful of villas occupied by City gentlemen who had retired there to enjoy life in the country. Five hundred men were employed at the railway works at Neasden, an indication of the new industry brought to the area. A few areas held out a little longer; even as late as 1882, the parish of Perivale had only some twenty inhabitants, but it lay only seven miles from Marble Arch, and its days were numbered.

South of the river, development was initially much slower, but here the railways eventually had perhaps an even greater impact, with the intricate network of suburban lines developed by the South-Eastern and Chatham, London, Brighton and South Coast and London and South Western Railways and their predecessors. Vast tracts of land, mostly unpopulated, were taken over for the two great junctions at Clapham and Bricklayers Arms. Croydon, served by two lines and no fewer than eleven stations at one time, increased its population from 6,000 in 1801 to 78,947 in 1881, becoming the largest suburban town in the neighbourhood of London. It was in Croydon that another new feature of suburban transport, the horse tramway, made its first appearance, running to Wandsworth. The later electric tramways, with their greater flexibility, gave the railways serious competition until the latter were themselves electrified after the Great War. Woolwich, always a busy town owing to its Army and Navy establishments, grew more steadily, but Plumstead, further down the line of the old North Kent Railway, increased rapidly to rival its neighbour in size. In 1800 there were only 200 houses in the whole parish; by 1851, however, the population was 8,000, and had risen to 33,000 thirty years later. The North Kent Railway was also the cause of the growth of the old village of Bexley: here, the new town, in contrast to others, had grown up on the coach road to Dover. The building of a station on the North Kent's loop line soon accelerated the growth of the old village, which saw its population quadruple in just

a few years.

Bromley, because it was an old, well-established town, did not feel the impact of the railway as immediately as did its neighbours Beckenham and Penge. The latter of these in particular, with the wide open spaces of its common to be used, became an important junction for the lines running east-west and north-south. With three stations, it grew from almost nothing in 1850 (Walford describes it as 'an unimportant country village with but one inn 'The Crooked Billet' the oldest house in Penge') to a town with a population of 180,000 in 1881, with several hotels, its own newspaper and, in a few years, several theatres. One town that resisted the coming of the railway for a while was Kingston-Upon-Thames. The nearest that its councillors would allow the line to approach was Surbiton, then a hamlet on the outskirts of the town. Almost instantly, Surbiton was transformed into a dormitory suburb: hardly had the station been completed than speculators had surrounded it with the geometric layout of streets that today's map shows. The building of a line to Kingston itself could not long be delayed, and a branch line, running through New Malden, was duly constructed. Houses mushroomed around the new station, which became known as New Kingston.

Sutton, Cheam and Ewell all had similar populations in 1851. The railway soon brought an influx of commuters, attracted by the pleasant countryside. Sutton showed the sharpest increase, from 1,100 in 1835 to around 9,000 in 1881. Cheam and Ewell roughly doubled in size. Their turn was to come in the twentieth century. Surrey was to escape the speculators' clutches for a few years yet; it is a remarkable fact that at the beginning of the nineteenth century one sixth of Surrey consisted of wild uncultivated heath and scrub.

The feelings of the old inhabitants of London's villages who lived through Victoria's reign must have been duplicated in this century by those of the old population's of towns like Harlow, Stevenage or Hemel Hempstead, or perhaps even more so by those engulfed by the growth of post-war Birmingham or Manchester. The decision to create the Green Belt came in the nick of time for Londoners, and luckily they can still get a breath of country air in the Surrey hills or Epping Forest.

Writing in 'Village London', Edward Walford, whose words were to be echoed by Percy Fitzgerald fifteen years later, had this to say of the Caterham Valley, for which he held a particular admiration, but the words apply to all the lost villages of London.

"Caterham Valley, which abuts upon Warlingham, and runs east and west about four miles to the south of Croydon, is, so far as it has escaped building operations, very rural and pretty. It is, however, as stated above, traversed by a branch line of railway; and it may be safely inferred, therefore, that it is only a question of time before green and smiling meadows will give place to rows of streets or villas with trim gardens. It has been truly remarked that London is almost daily growing. First come the long monotonous lines of streets and houses, extending on every side, and pushing out arms and feelers in the direction of the country. But far beyond these the builder is busy at his work. He has to meet the wants and wishes of men who seek to combine the advantages of London and of country life. There is a large and increasing class who are not content to be Londoners in the old sense of the word. They must have more space and elbow-room than the close neighbourhood of London can afford. They are impatient of life in a street, and they are driven every year farther and farther afield in search of open and unoccupied ground. In these days of rapid railway communication there is hardly any spot safe from them within reasonable distance of town. They will fix themselves anywhere, so only that there is a railway-station not too far off; and there are very few of the outlying suburbs of London which are not thus suitable for them. But where they settle the charms of the country disappear. What was lately a field is enclosed, and becomes a garden or a private park, from which the public are shut out. Forests are cut down to make room for the new occupants, or are left standing only as far as they are ornamental appendages to the property. This is the sort of process which has been going on for many years past on all sides of London. We may like or dislike it, but we can raise no objection to it. We must take it as part of the general growth of London, and, so viewed, it rises almost to the dignity of a natural law. All that we can ask is that some limits may be assigned to it—that some spots of ground here and there may be kept sacred from intrusion, and may be protected from the flood which is overwhelming all around them."

Every city dweller will, we are sure, say Amen to Walford's words of a century ago.

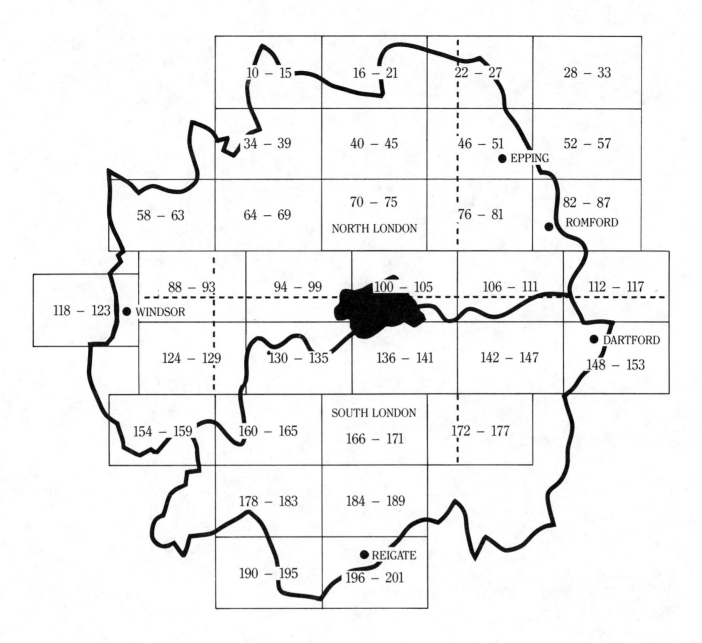

10 – 15	16 – 21	22 – 27	28 – 33
34 – 39	40 – 45	46 – 51	52 – 57
			● EPPING	

58 – 63   64 – 69   70 – 75 NORTH LONDON   76 – 81   82 – 87 ROMFORD

118 – 123 ● WINDSOR   88 – 93   94 – 99   100 – 105   106 – 111   112 – 117

124 – 129   130 – 135   136 – 141   142 – 147   148 – 153 ● DARTFORD

154 – 159   160 – 165   SOUTH LONDON 166 – 171   172 – 177

178 – 183   184 – 189

190 – 195   196 – 201   ● REIGATE

The Maps

Publisher's Note

The maps in this Atlas are based on a scale of two inches to the mile. However, because of the number of different maps involved and the reproduction thereof there may be some minor variations in scale. The age of the maps and the fact that there could be as much as fifteen years difference between the dates of survey of adjoining maps, plus the handling and folding which has taken place over the years, have also meant that there are small differences here and there which are impossible to eradicate.

The publishers have made every effort to minimise these faults and trust the reader will make allowances for any slight imperfections.

10

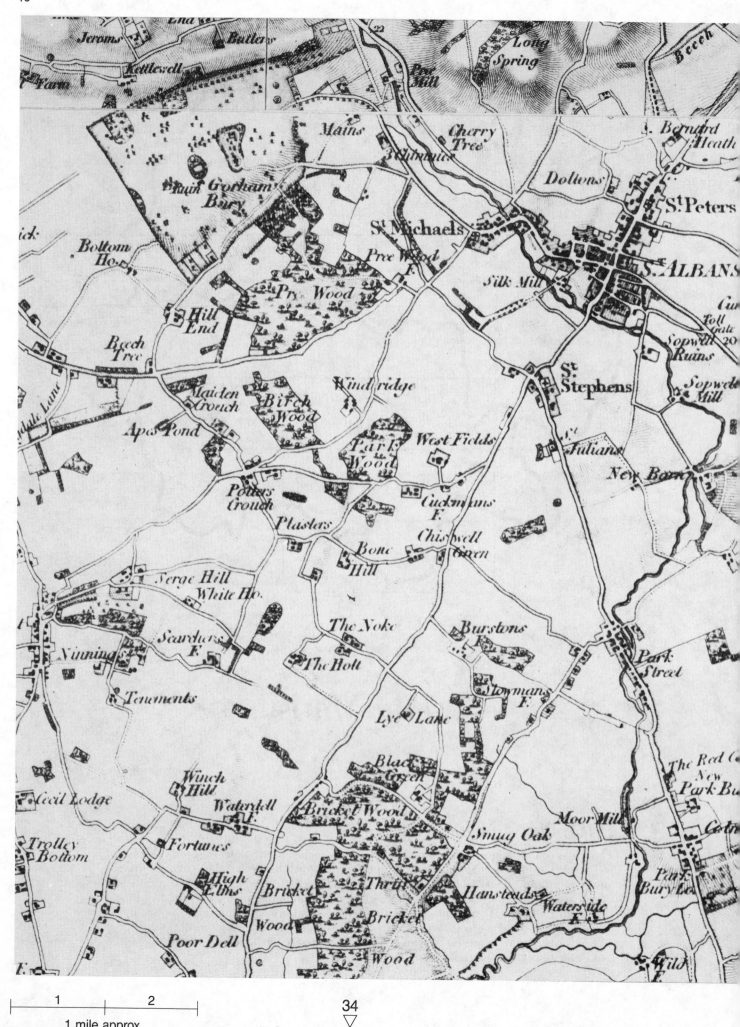

1   2

1 mile approx.

34
▽

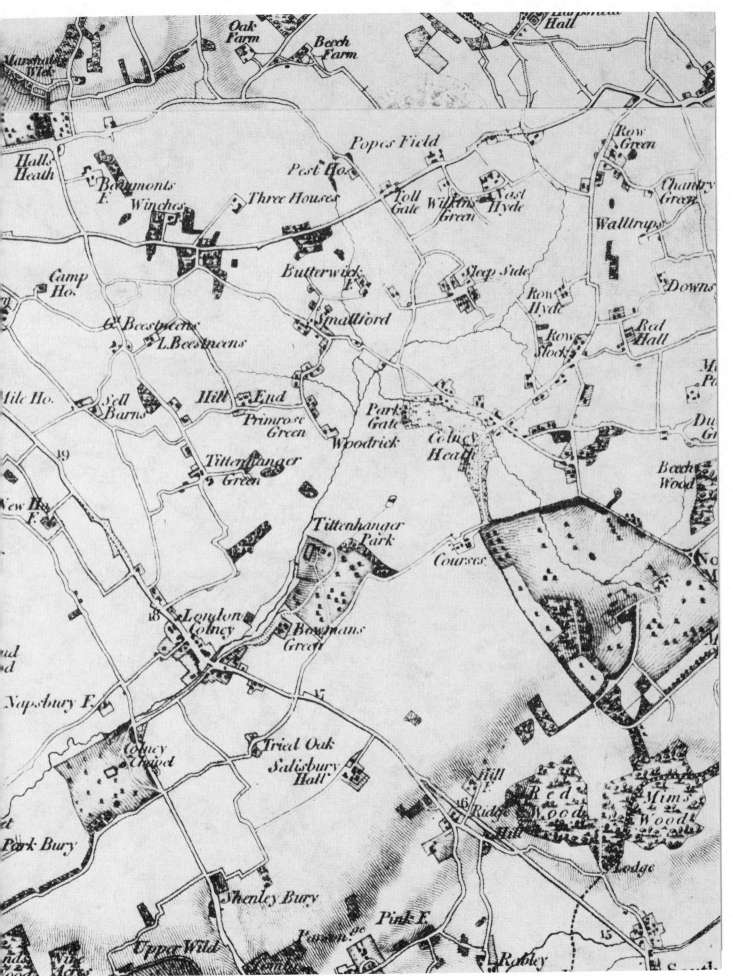

16 ▷

Published 1822.

12

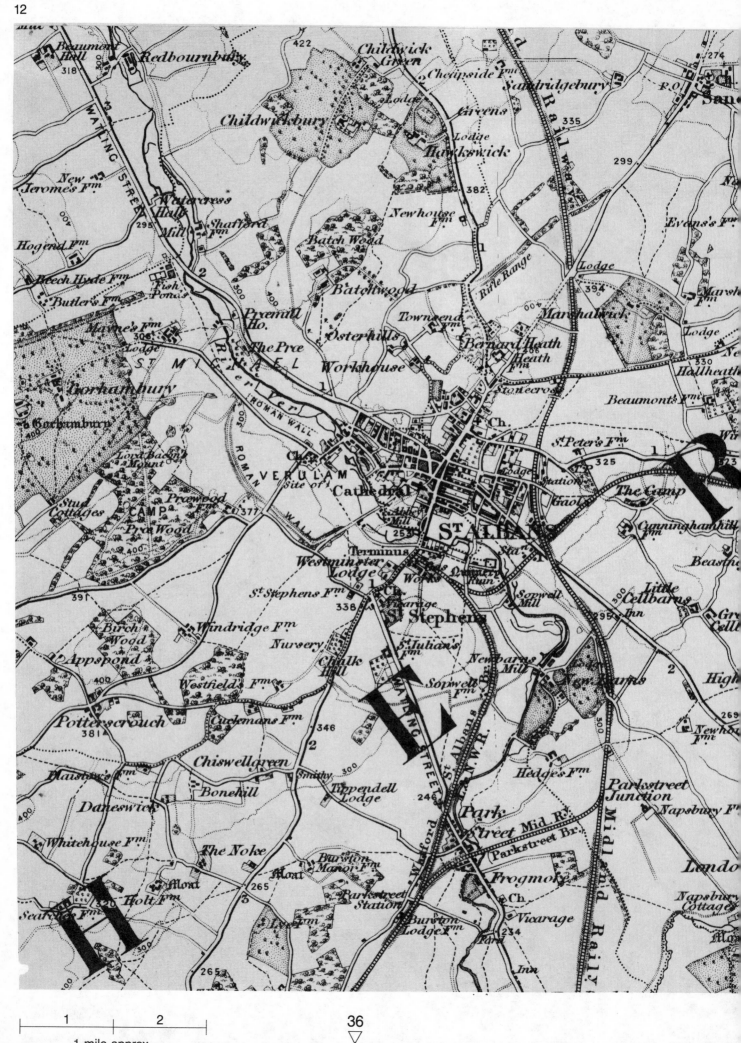

Great Wood

Furze Field

Sutton's Fm

Fairfoals Fm

Hook's Fm

Moat

Astwick Manor

Cooper's Green

Birchwood Fm

Woodhall Fm

256

245

200

Mount Pleasant

Lodge

Oak Fm

Beech Fm

Harpsfield Hall

Pattocksock

Workhouse

New Town

Gas Works

271

Station

HATFI

262

250 4

Ellenbrook

Rectory

Roe Green

Lawnr Ho.

Lodge

Hatfield

Hatfi

Coo Wood

241

Popefield Fm

Lodge

The Horseshoes

3

Inn

Oaklands

250

Wilkin's Green

Smallford Station

Gt. N.

Hatfield

PETER

Hally

St. Albans Br.

256

300

290

Roehyde Fm

Downs Fm

Travellers Fm

Millwar

Par

Hollybush Hall

Redhouse Fm

Sleepshyde

Redhall Fm

296

18▷

Marshmoor

The Bush

Smallford

231

Ch.

Roundhouse Fm

245

Roestock

Angerland Common

Bullen's Green

Parsonage Fm

Delsome Bottom

School

Hillend Fm

Rectory

Parkgate Corners

School

Bush Wood

P.O.

Welham Green Inn

Tyttenhanger Green

77

COLNEY HEATH

T.P.

Tollgate Fm

249

29

Moat

Pancakehall

R. Colne

Tyttenhanger Fm

Kennels

Lodge

North Mimms

Potterells

Ford

Lo

280

Coursers Fm

Tyttenhanger Park

North Mimms

ch.

Lodge

245

267

239

Park

Water End

308

Bowmansgreen

Lodge

Walsingham Wood

Abdale Ho.

School

ney

Cobs Ash

Hawkshead Ho.

Inn 4

252

Potwells

Hawkshead Wood

256

oad olney

ney Ho.

Salisbury

Moat Hall

Ridgehill Fm

Redwell

Lodge

Mimmshall

228

Lodge

300

Surveyed 1865-1880. Published 1887.

1 mile approx.

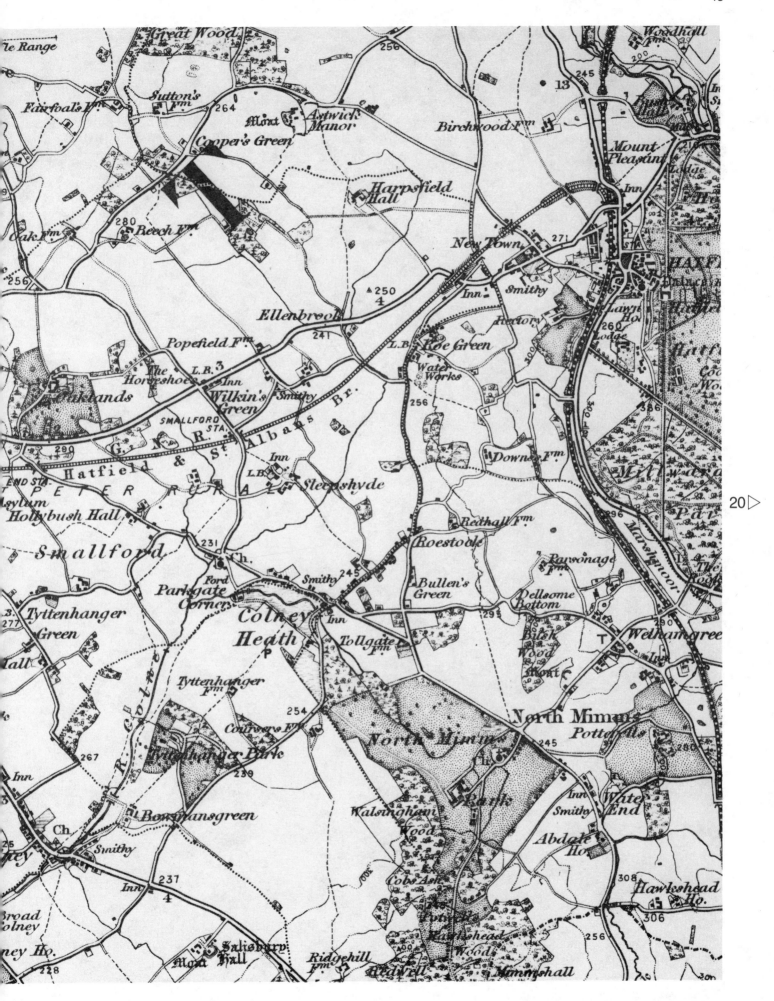

Surveyed 1865-1880. Revised 1902. Published 1904.

ATFIELD

Parson.^{ge}

Rye
End

Kiln

West End

Essenden
Bury

ESSENDEN

Bedwell F.

19

H a t f i e l d

Hoxleys
Pond

Popes

Kibes
Gwn

Bedwell

Park

Ber
st

Hog
Lane

Upper
Woodride

Wild Hill

Purta
Place

Camfield
Pla.

Bedwell
Lodge

Woode
Lo

Cucumber
Hall

rs
rsonage

Marsh
Moor

Low.
Woodride

Grubs Lane

Georges
Wood

Wood
End

sham
en

Foxes

Bell

Cold Harbour

11

Skimpans

Bar

Kentish
Lane

Barbers
Lodge

Welham
Green

rth
ms

Potterells

Brockman

Park

8 Miles from
Hertford

New I

Sheepshead
Hall

Murie

Shephards F.

s
eet

Gobions

Hawks Head

Friday
Grove

Swanley
Bar

Lodge

Warren
Gate

Reeves

Leggats

Boltons

Little
Heath

Brick
Kilns

Darks F.

Mims Hall

Honey
Wood

Clock
Ho.

The Hook

Northaw

Cooper Lane

Park F.^{rm}

Willets
F.

T.P.

1   2

1 mile approx.

22▷

Bayford Hall

Bayford

Observatory

Bayford Green

Brickington Green

Epping Green

Ashina Grove

Outer Claypits

Etridge Cross

Wormley

Wood

Punsborn

Park

Lodge

Punsborn F. St Lawrence E.

Dorrys Wood

Long Grove

Newgate Street

Tallsmores

Limekiln

Hanyards

Goughs Oak

Cooileys

Sopers E.

Love Grove

Burnt F.m

Box Wood

Wades F.m

Goose Gr.

Hoddesdon Park Wood

Broxbourn Wood

Broxbourn Park

Little Wood

Gate

Wormley West End

Wormley Bury

Bases F.m

Beaumont Gr.

Cheshunt

Appleburv Street

New R

Flamstead End

Cheshunt Street

Hammond Street

Canna Hill

Cheshunt

13

Love Grove

Turners Hill

Published 1822.

241

202

217

238

Eastend Green

Roxford

Mo

River Lea

Hollwell F^m

Woodmers Park

200

148

Upper Mill

Lodges

Cecil Mill

Essendonbury

Mill

Water Hall

150

Bunkers Hill

200

The Vineyard

e Park

236

200

How Green

Kennel Ho.

Bayford Hall

332

Smithy

ESSENDON

Ch.

Lodge

Pondfield Ho.

Bay

Lower Westend

West End

272

Bedwellpark
F^m

Little

347

Bayford

300

Morrelhill
Brickkiln

Hilland F^m

Little
Berkhampstead
Ho.

Berkhampstead

Wood

Lodge

380

eld Park

Essendon Place Lodge

Bedwell Park

Lodge

Ch.

55

N

Pope's F^m

363

300

Buck's F^m

Bedwell Lodge
F^m

Bush F^m

Blackfan F^m

Green Street

Cattfield
Place

Cumber
Hall

Woodcote F^m

Epping
Mon^t

P.O.

Epping Green

ter

Woodside Place

385

13

Lodge

Woodside

Wildhill

Warrenwood

376

Lodge

Moat

Tyler's Causeway

Lower
Woodside

Lo

Lodge

78

300

400

Lodge

Fox's

359

Woodhill

Ch.

Woodfield

Moat

Coalharbour
F^m

414

Lodge

School

369

2½

Kentishlane
F^m

Barberslodge F^m

Newpark F^m

Vicarage

400

Ch.

Till Bay
Lodge

400

P.O.

Newgate Street

Lodge

Brookmans

Great
Wood

397

Justice Hill

Great Wood

Brook

Tolmer

Moffats
Park

3½

Grims

411

Home
Wood

200

300

289

Minwood
Ho.

Well
Wood

Woodlands

The Ridgeway

Manor

370

Hanyards F^m

Lodge

Reeves F^m

Lodge

339

Legatts F^m

Lodge

Wyn Park

Lodge

Brickkiln
F^m

Cuffl

*Cuffley
Hills*

Bolton's
F^m

Legatts

Lodge

4½

Northaw

School

Hemps
Hill

+ Site of
Kings Well

School

1   2

1 mile approx.

Bayfordbury

Brickendon Bury

Ducketts Wood

Blakesfield

Clements

Elbowlane Fm

Dalmonds

Jepps

Sewards

Monk's Green

Warren Ho

Highfield Wood

Bayford Place Fm

Fanshaws

Hacketts

Brickendon Green

Cowheath Wood

Brickendon Grange

Broxbourne Wood

Claypits

Kilrage Fm

Cold Hall

Benram Wood

Emanuel Pollards

Carneles Green

West Lea

Manor

West End

Wormley Wood

Beaumont Manor

Thunderfield Grove

Tanfield Fm

St Lawrence Fm

Appleby Street

Hammond Street

Burton Grange

Windmill

Lucas End

Pantilehall

Goffs Oak

Reynoldsgreen

Claramont

Poyndon Pits

Coles Grove

Harleybury College

Woollensbrooke

Woollens Brook Wood

Westfield

Highleigh Fm

HODDESDON

High Leigh

Hoddesdonpark Wood

Ford

Hoddesdon Bury

Broxbourne Bury

Broxbourne

Bads Hill

The Paws

Wormleyhill Fm

Lodge

Wormleybury

Wormley

Factory Fm

Moat

Nunsbury

Turnford

Cheshunt Park

Roundcroft

Brookfield Fm

Mill Lane Fm

Reservoir

Flamstead End

Reservoir

Site of CAMP

Cheshunt Street

Gews Corner

Chesnut Green Ho

River Lea

Cambridge Line Gt En Ry

River Lea Navigation

24 ▷

Surveyed 1865-1880. Published 1887.

◁15

1   2

1 mile approx.

Surveyed 1865-1880. Revised 1902. Published 1904.

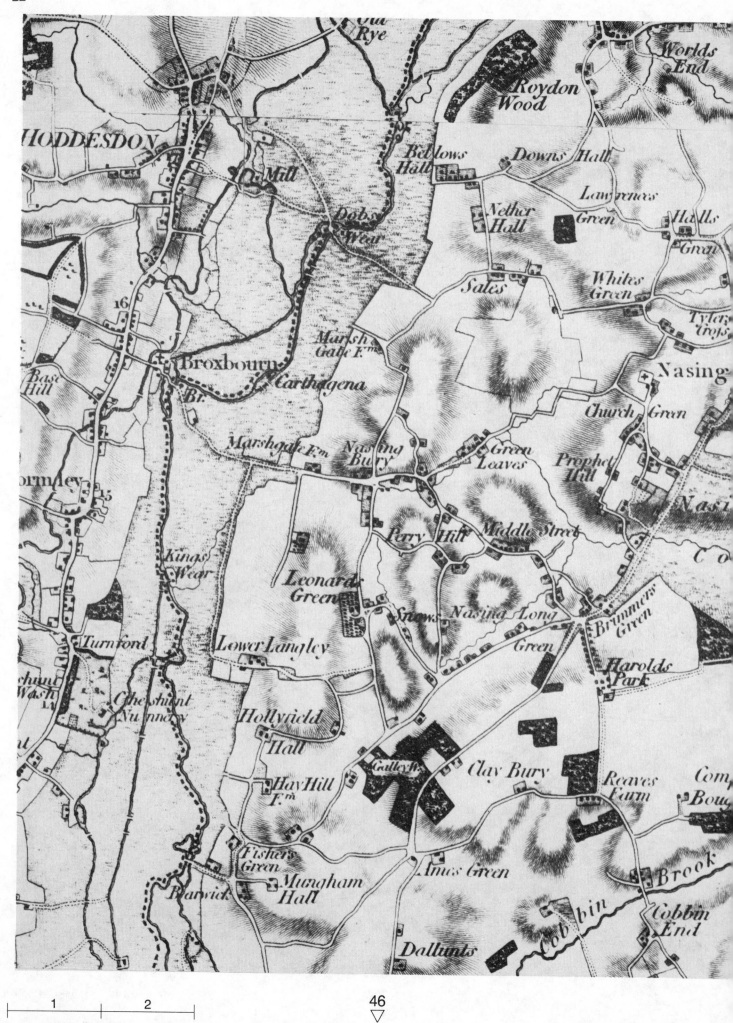

HODDESDON

Old Rye

Roydon Wood

Worlds End

Bellows Hall

Downs Hall

Mill

Lawrences Green

Nether Hall

Halls Green

Dobbs Wear

Sales

Whites Green

16

Marsh Gate F.m

Nasing

Base Hill

Broxbourn

Carthagena

Church Green

Br.

Tylers Cross

Marshgate F.m

Nasing Bury

Green Leaves

Prophet Hill

ormley

15

Nasi

17

Perry Hill

Middle Street

Kings Wear

Co

Leonard Green

Snows

Nasing Long

Brummers Green

Turnford

Lower Langley

Green

Harolds Park

eshunt Wash

Cheshunt Nunnery

Hollyfield Hall

Galley W.k

Clay Bury

Reaves Farm

Com Bough

Hay Hill F.m

Fishers Green

Amos Green

Brook

Arwick

Mungham Hall

Dallunts

Cobbin

Cobbin End

1   2

1 mile approx.

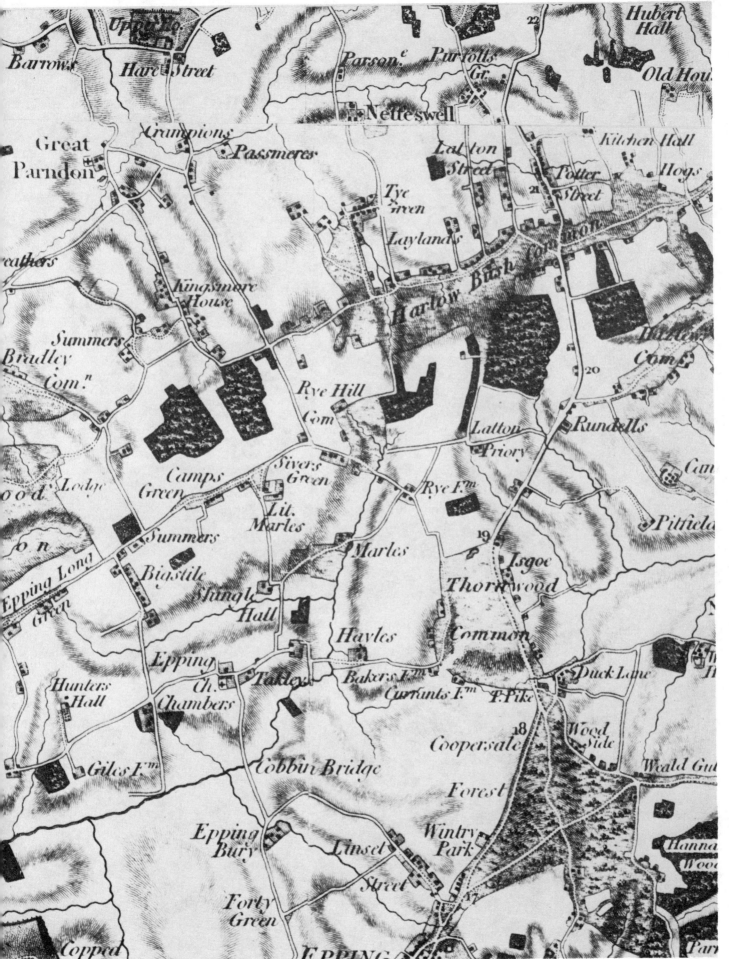

Barrows

Upper He

Hare Street

Parson^e

Purfolts Gr.

Netteswell

Hubert Hall

Old Hou

Great Parndon

Cramptons

Passmeres

Latton Street

Kitchen Hall

Hogs

Potter Street

Tye Green

22

21

eathers

Kingsmore House

Laylands

Harlow Bush Common

Summers

Bradley Com.^n

Rye Hill Com

20

Harlow Com

Latton Priory

Rundells

Camps Green

Sivers Green

Rye F.^m

Lit. Marles

19

Can

28 ▷

Pittfiela

Summers

Marles

Isgoe

Lodge

Bigstile

Thornwood

ood

Epping Long Green

Bungle Hall

Hayles

Common

Hunters Hall

Epping

Takley

Bakers F.^m

Duck Lane

Woodside

Weald Gut

on

Ch. Chambers

Currants F.^m

T. Pike

18

Coopersale

Giles F.^m

Cobbin Bridge

Forest

Wintry Park

Hanna Wood

Epping Bury

Linsel

Street

Copped

Forty Green

EPPING

47 ▽

Published 1805.

◁ 19

1   2

1 mile approx.

Surveyed 1869-1878. Published 1886.

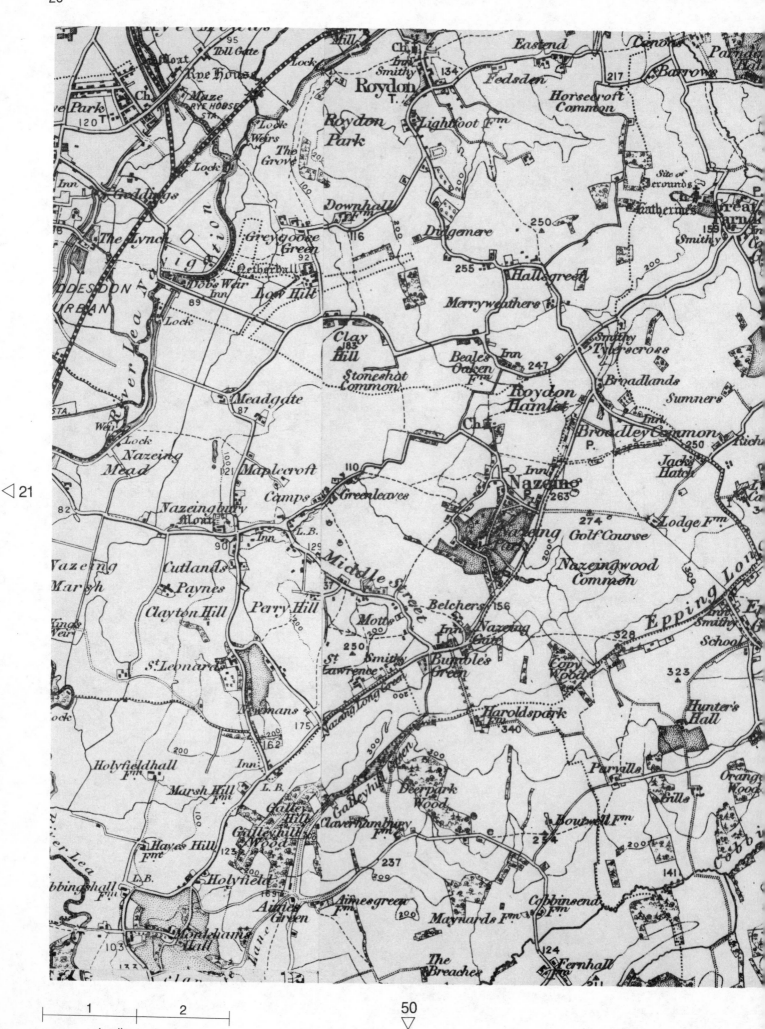

1   2

1 mile approx.

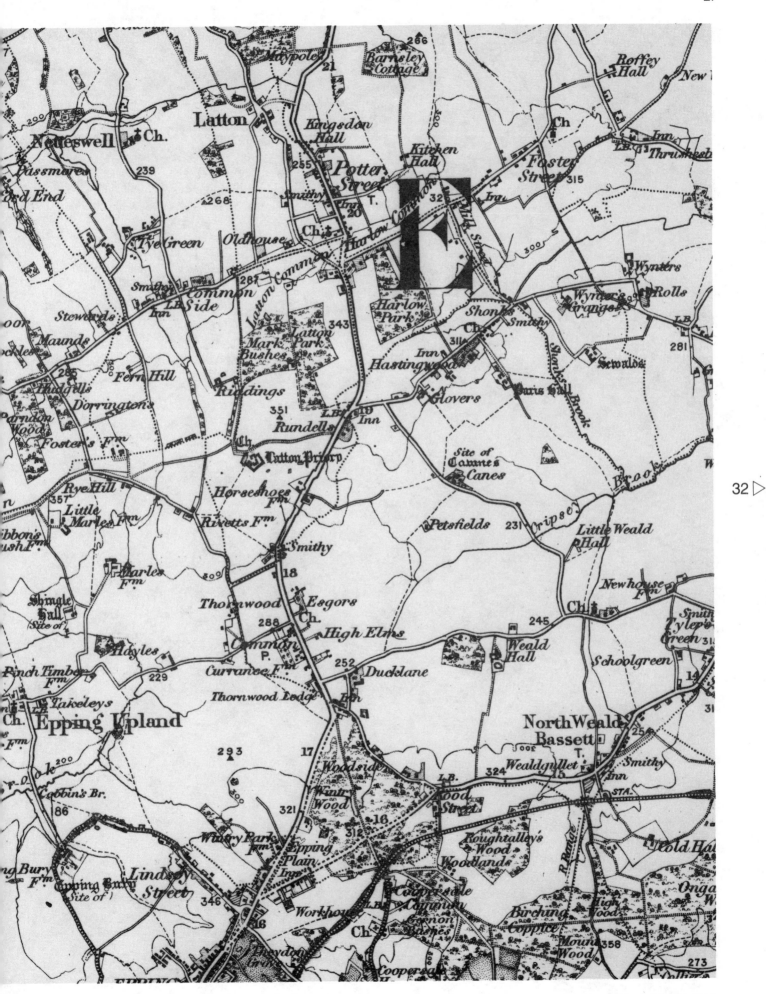

32 ▷

Surveyed 1869-1878. Revised 1902-1903. Published 1905.

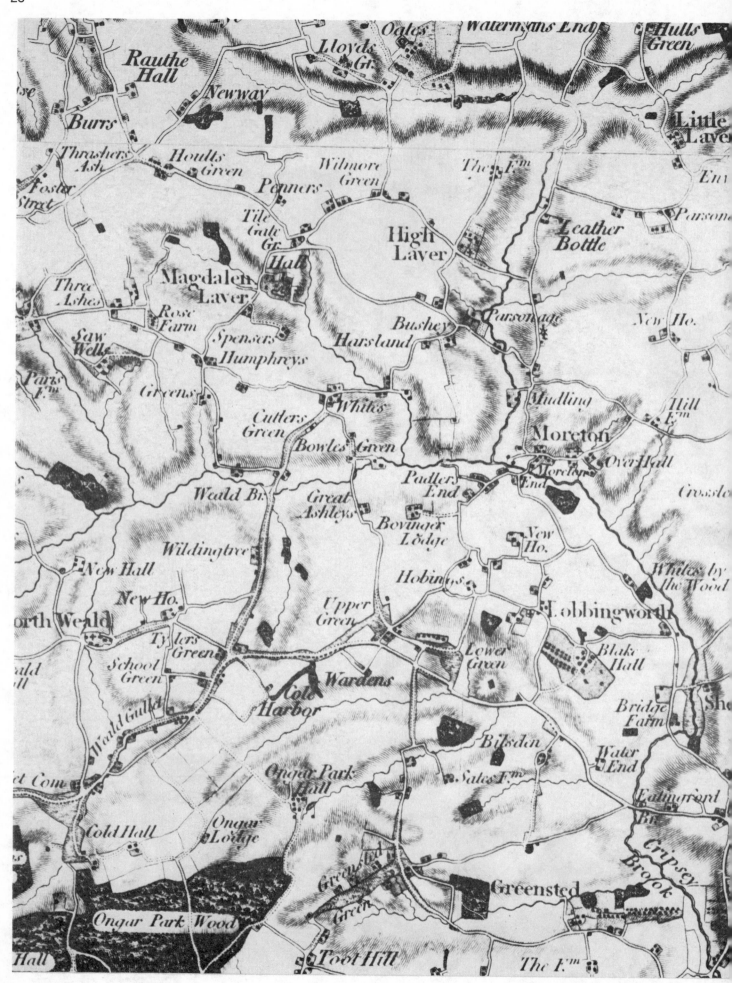

Rauthe Hall

Newway

Burrs

Thrashers Ash

Foster Street

Hoults Green

Penners

Tile Gate Gr.

Three Ashes

Magdalen Laver

Rose Farm

Saw Wells

Paris Fm

Spensers

Humphreys

Greens

Cutlers Green

Bowles Green

Weald Br.

Wildingtree

New Hall

New Ho.

orth Weald

Tylers Green

School Green

eald ll

Weald Gullet

ret Com

Cold Hall

Ongar Lodge

Ongar Park Wood

Hall

Mole Harbor

Wardens

Ongar Park Hall

Great Ashleys

Upper Green

Whites

Harsland

Bushey

High Laver

Lloyds Gr.

Oates

Watermans End

Little Laver

Wilmore Green

The Fm

Leather Bottle

Parsonage

New Ho.

Mudling

Moreton

Padlers End

Bovinger Lodge

Hobings

New Ho.

Lobbingworth

Lower Green

Blake Hall

Bilsden

Sales Fm

Bridge Farm

Water End

Ealingfront

Greensted

Cripsey Brook

Toot Hill

The Fm

Greensted Green

Over Hall

Whites by the Wood

Crosslet

Hulls Green

Env

Parson

Hill Fm

Moreton End

◁ 23

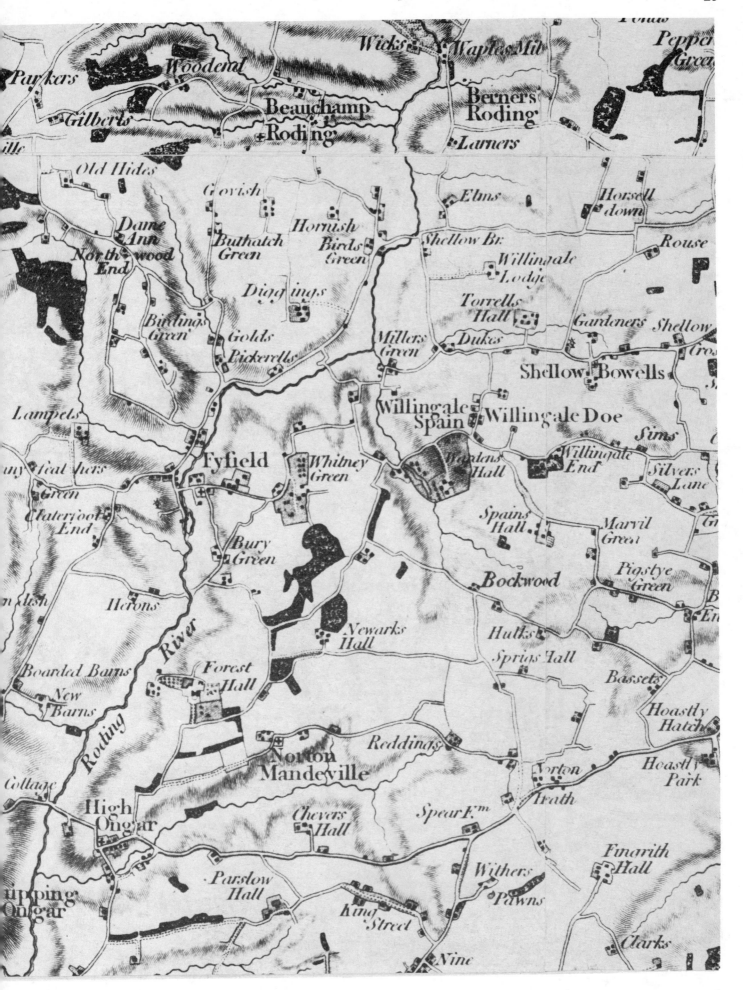

Published 1805.

1 mile approx.

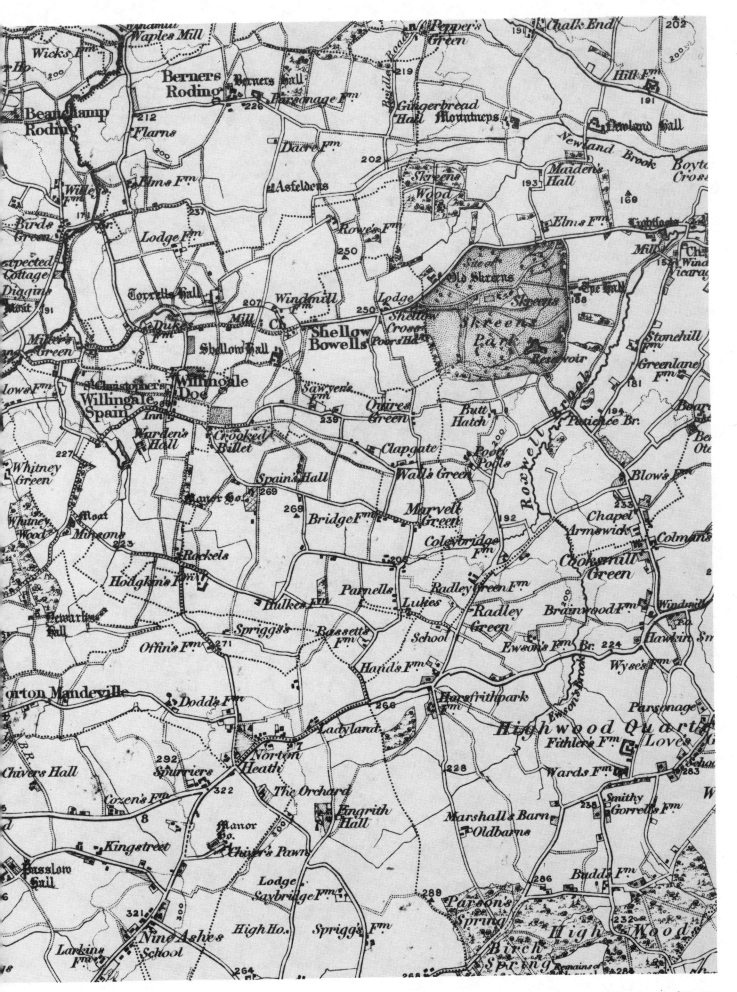

Surveyed 1869-1878. Published 1886.

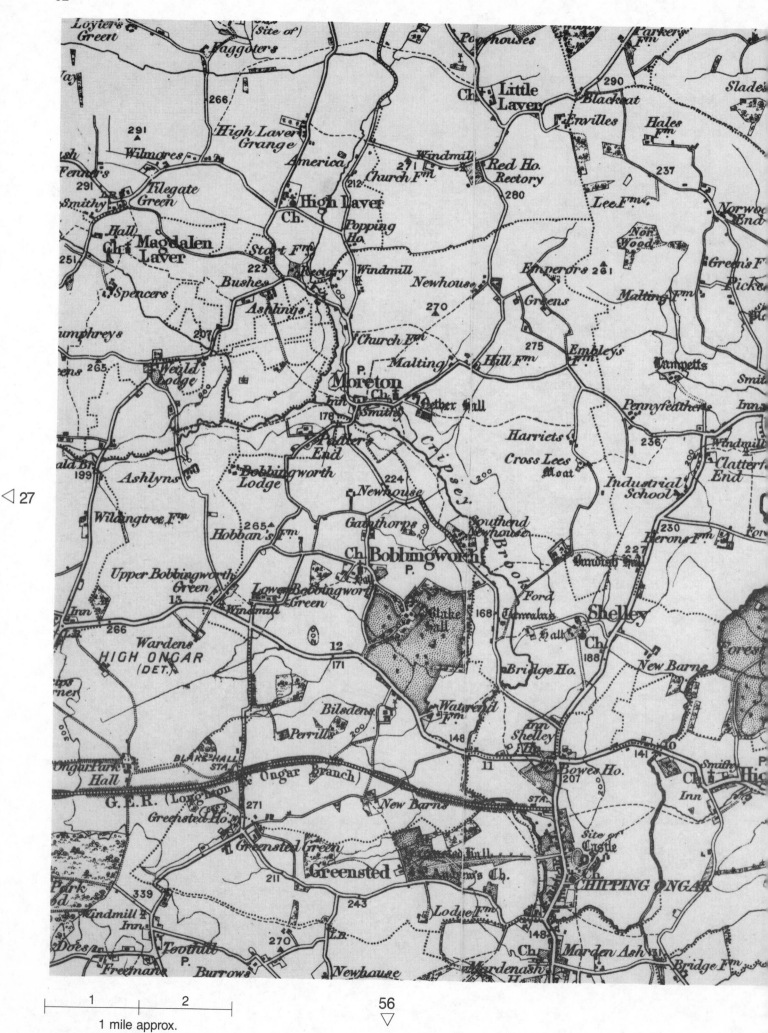

◁ 27

1   2

1 mile approx.

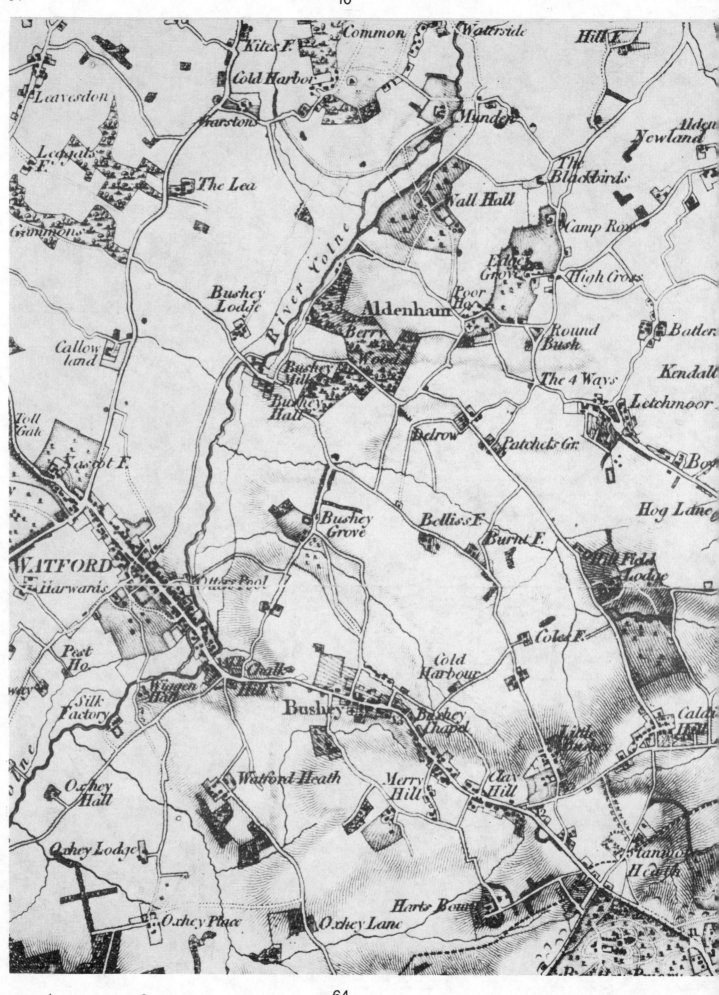

1 2

1 mile approx.

Published 1822.

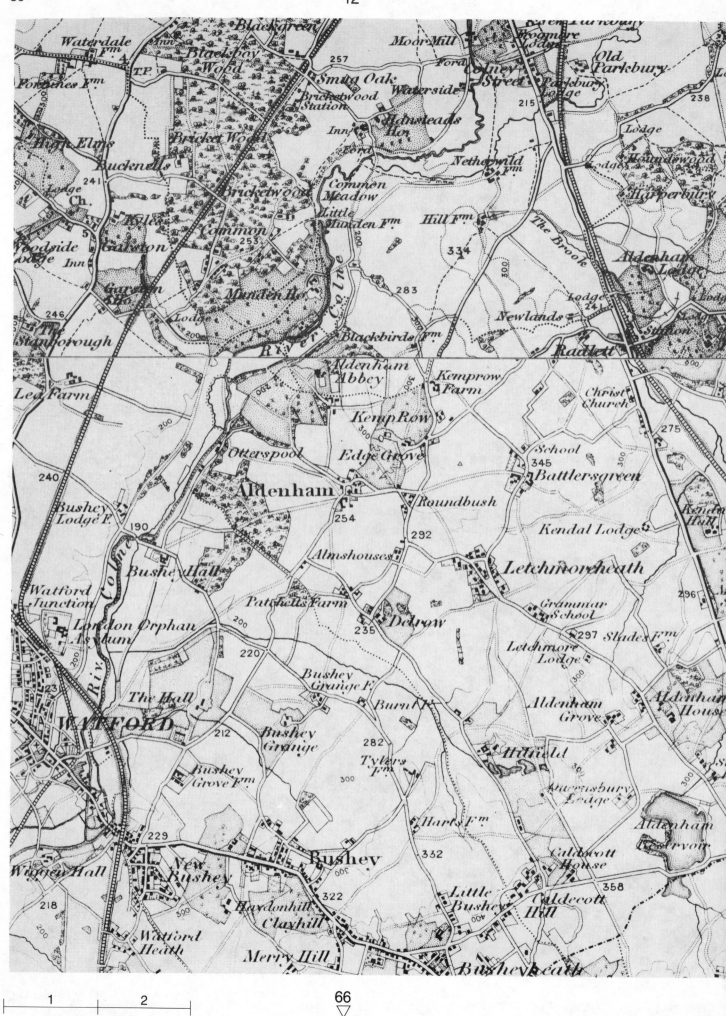

1   2

1 mile approx.

Surveyed 1862-1880. Published 1887.

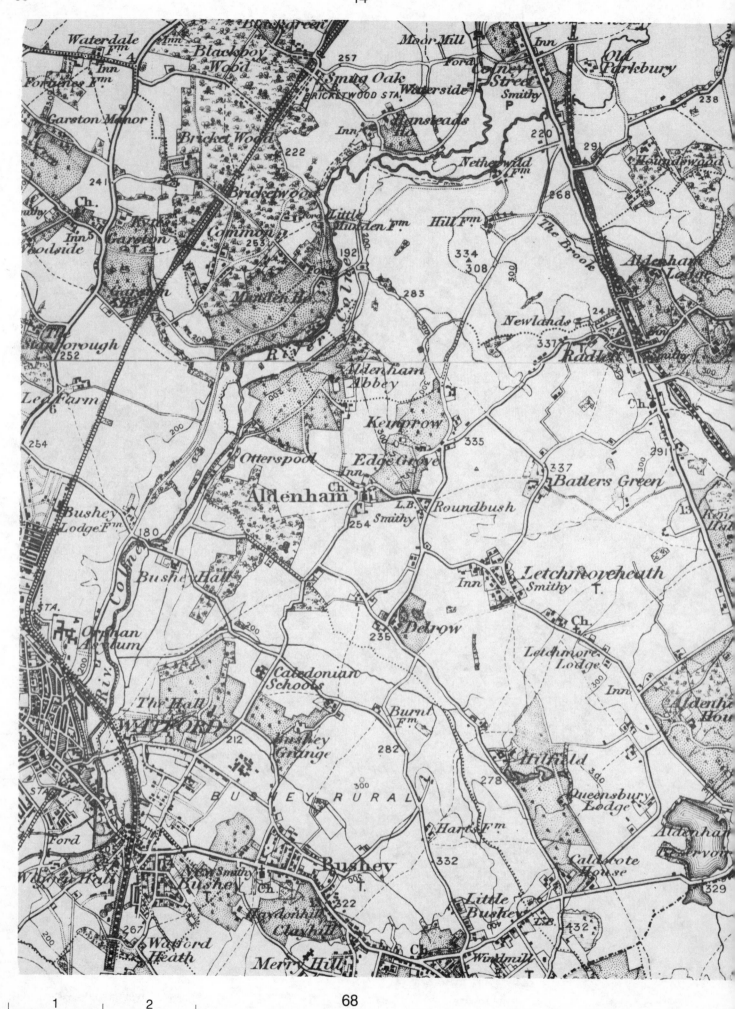

1   2

1 mile approx.

Surveyed 1862-1880. Revised 1902. Published 1904.

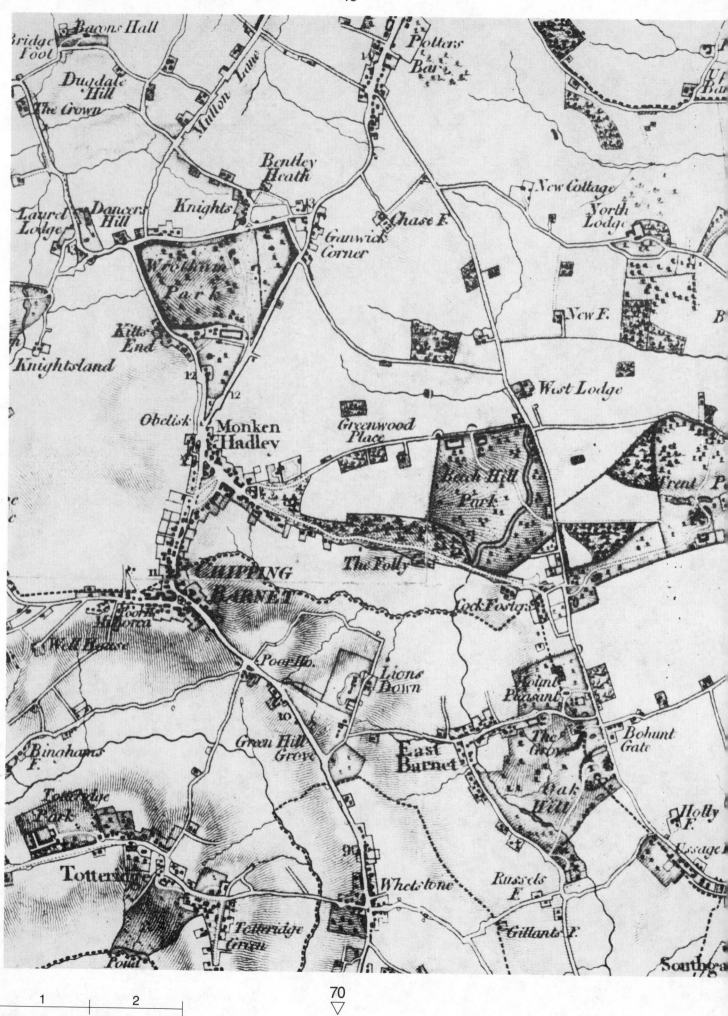

1   2

1 mile approx.

Published 1822.

1 mile approx.

48▷

Surveyed 1862-1880. Published 1887.

◁39

1   2

1 mile approx.

Surveyed 1862-1880. Published 1887.

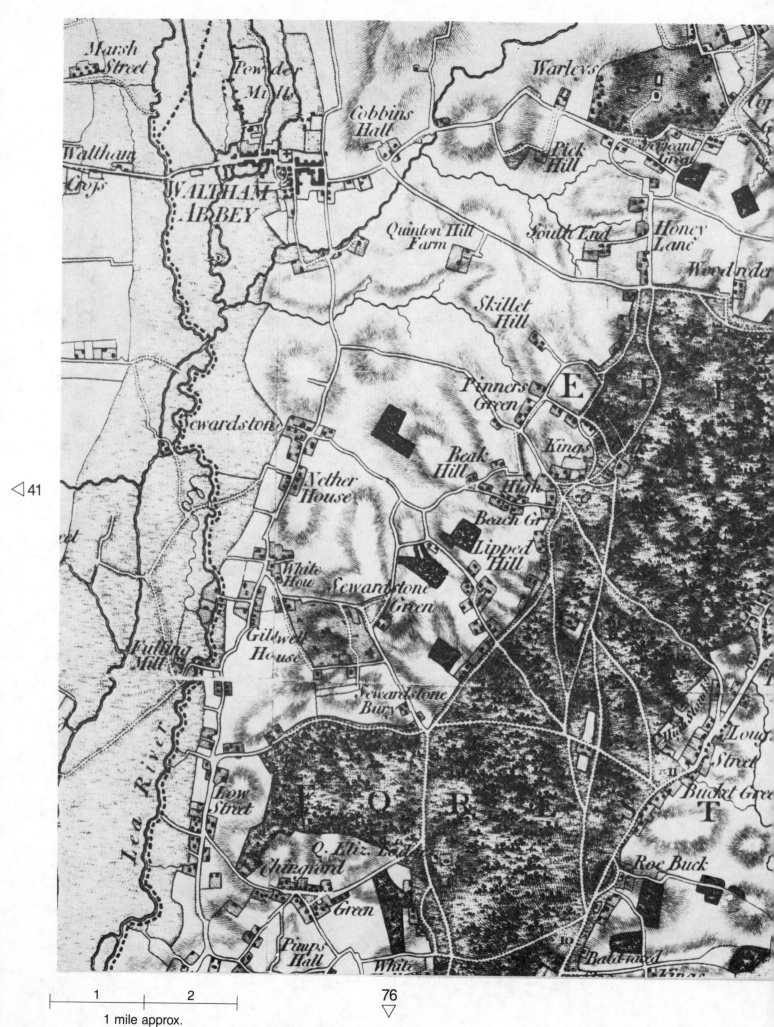

46

△
22

◁ 41

Marsh Street

Powder Mills

Waltham Crofs

WALTHAM ABBEY

Cobbins Hall

Warleys

Pick Hill

Sergeant Green

Quinton Hill Farm

South End

Honey Lane

Wood reder

Skillet Hill

Pinners Green

E

Sewardston

Beak Hill

Kings

High

Nether House

Beach Gr

Lipped Hill

White Hou

Sewardstone Green

Gilwell House

Fulling Mill

Sewardstone Bury

Lea River

Low Street

O R T

Itch Wood

Loug Street

Bucket Gree

T

Roe Buck

Q. Eliz. Lodge

Chingford

Green

Pimps Hall

White

Bald faced

10

1   2

1 mile approx.

76
▽

Published 1805.

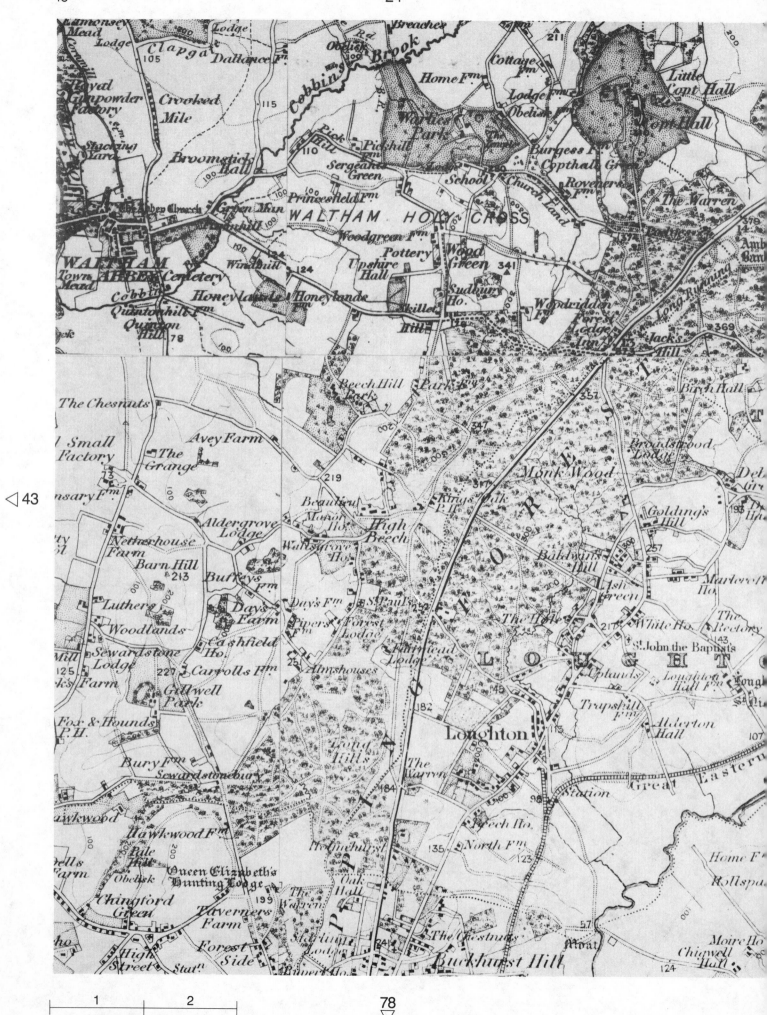

◁43

54 ▷

Surveyed 1862-1873. Published 1883.

56 ▷

Surveyed 1862-1873. Revised 1903. Published 1904.

1   2

1 mile approx.

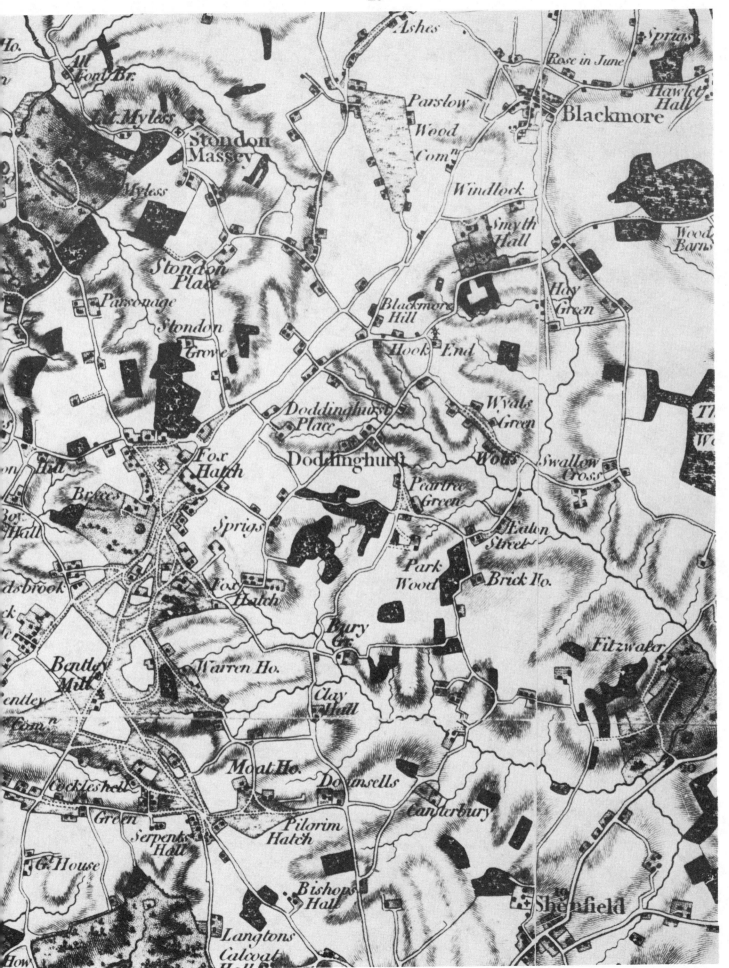

Ho.

All Font Br.

Lt. Myles

Stondon Massey

Myles

Stondon Place

Parsonage

Stondon Grove

Doddinghurst Place

Fox Hatch

Doddinghurst

Brices

Sprigs

Fox Hatch

Warren Ho.

Bentley Mill

Bentley

Com'n

Cockleshell Green

Serpents Hall

G. House

How

Moat Ho.

Downsells

Pilgrim Hatch

Bishops Hall

Langtons

Calcoat

Bury Gr.

Clay Hall

Canterbury

Ashes

Parslow Wood Com'n

Windlock

Smyth Hall

Blackmore Hill

Hook End

Wyats Green

Wous

Peartree Green

Park Wood

Eaton Street

Brick Ho.

Sprigs

Rose in June

Hawlet Hall

Blackmore

Hay Green

Wood Barns

Swallow Cross

Th Wo

Fitzwater

Shenfield

Published 1805.

1   2

1 mile approx.

Surveyed 1862-1873. Published 1883.

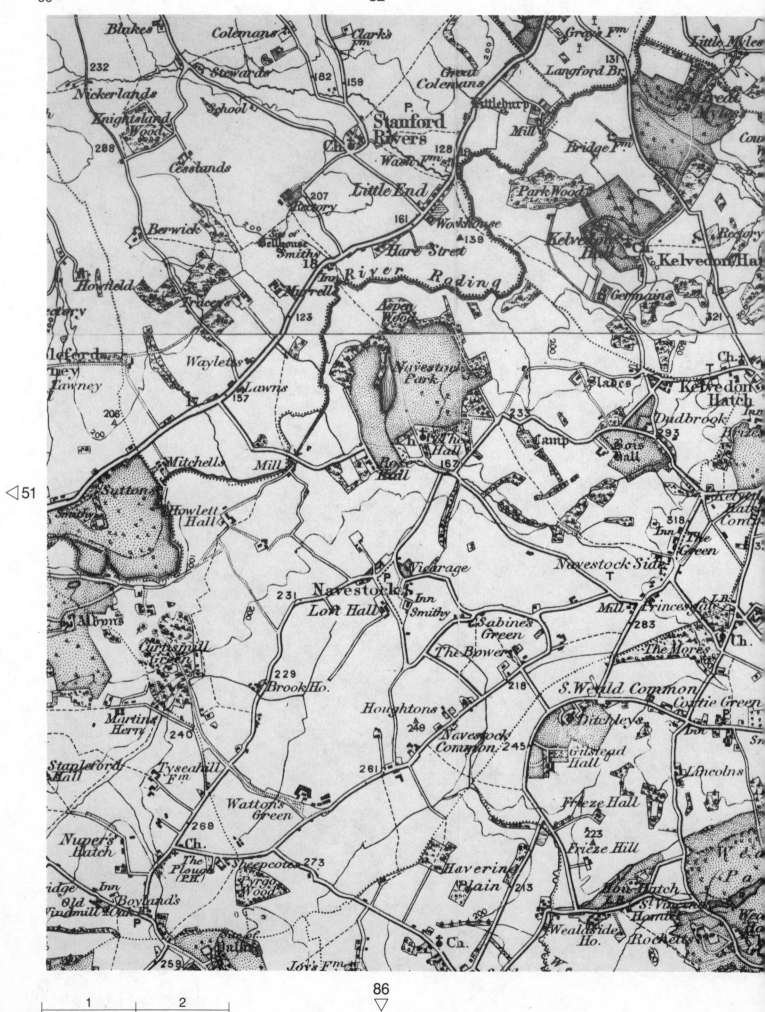

Blakes
Colemans
Clark's Fm
Grays Fm
Little Myles
Stewards
232
182
159
Langford Br
131
Nickerlands
Great Colemans
Knightsland Wood
School
P.
288
Rattlebury
Stanford Rivers
Mill
Bridge Fm
Cesslands
Ch.
128
Park Wood
Rectory
207
Wash Fm
19
Berwick
Little End
Kelvedon
200
161
Rectory
Site of Bellhouse
Smithy
Workhouse
139
Kelvedon Hall
18
Hare Street
Howfield
Murrell
River Roding
St Germains
Braces
Inn
123
Aspen Wood
321
Waylets
Navestock Park
Slades
Kelvedon Hatch
Tawney
Lawns
157
Dudbrook
293
206
200
Camp
Bois Hall
Mitchells
Mill
Ch. The Hall
233
Sutton
Rose Hall
167
51
Howlett Hall
318
Kelvedon Hatch Comm
Inn
The Green
Vicarage
Navestock Side
T
231
Navestock
Inn
Albyns
Lost Hall
Smithy
Mill
Princes
Curtismill Green
Sabines Green
283
The Mores
The Bower
229
218
S. Weald Common
Brook Ho.
Cottie Green
Houghtons
Ditchleys
249
Martins Hern
240
Navestock Common
245
Gilstead Hall
Lincolns
Stapleford Hall
Tyseahall Fm
261
Frieze Hall
Watton's Green
269
223
Frieze Hill
Nuper's Hatch
Ch.
Sheepcotes
273
Havering Plain
243
Fox Hatch
The Plough (P.H.)
Pyrgo Wood
St Vincents
Bridge
Inn
200
Wealdside Ho.
Rockett
Old Windmill
Oak
Boyland's
259
Joys Fm
Ch.

1   2
1 mile approx.

Surveyed 1862-1873. Revised 1903. Published 1904.

1 mile approx.

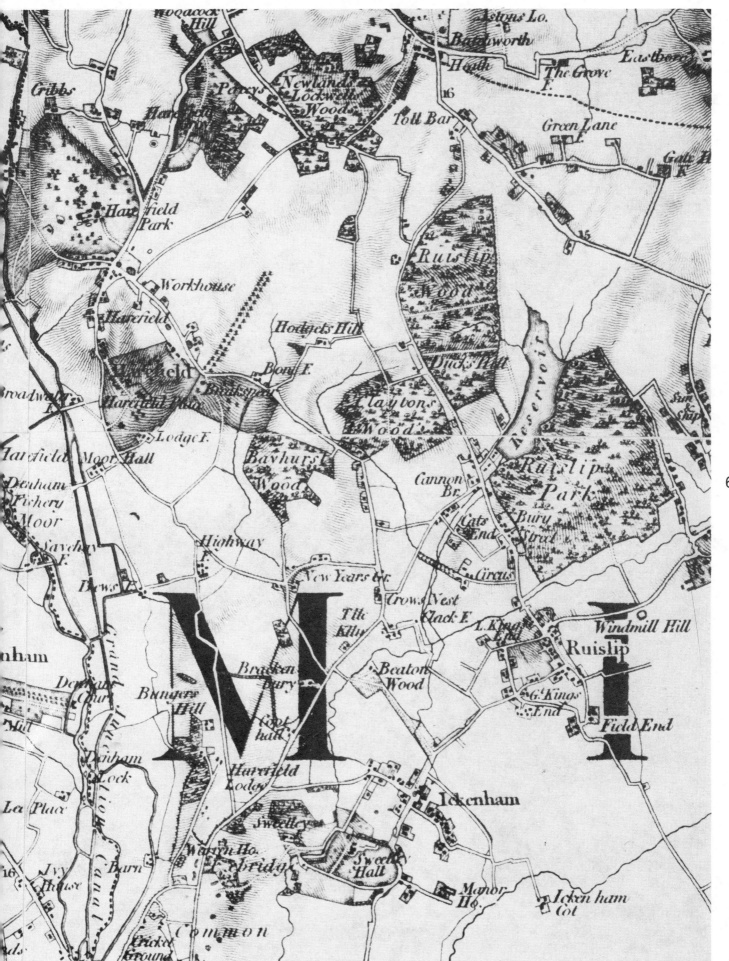

64 ▷

Published 1822.

1 mile approx.

Surveyed 1863-1876. Published 1880.

1   2

1 mile approx.

Surveyed 1863-1876. Revised 1902. Published 1904.

Oxhey Lane

Burnt Oak

Kiln

Pinner Wood

Pinner Hill

Brooks Hill

Weald Park

Woodready

Dove Ho. Fm

Wood Hall

Hatch End

Weald Stone

Pinner Grove

Harrow Weald

14

Pinner Park

Harrow F.

T.P.

Pinner

Haulstone Fm

Pinner Green

West End

Eastcot

12

Eastcot Ho. Field

Pinner Grove

Hooking Green

Greenhill

High Grove

End

11

T.Pike

D

Great Hill Lodge

Sheepcote F.

Harrow on the Hill

New F.

The Hermitage

Flambard

Sudbury Grove

Roxeth

The

New House

Sudbury

Wood End

Greenford

Green

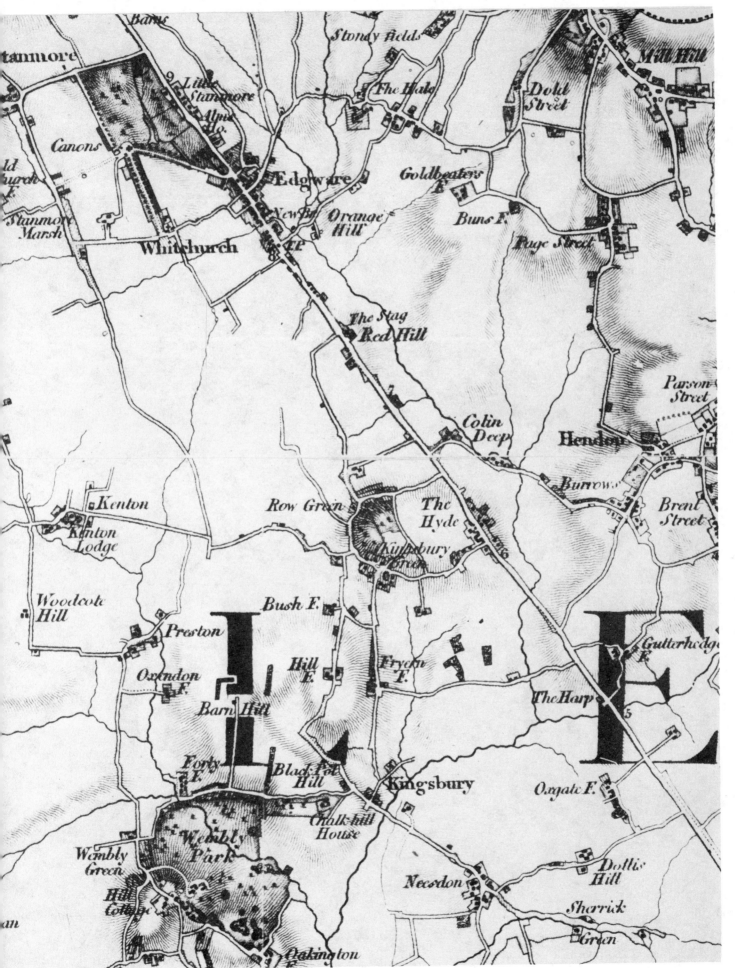

70▷

Published 1822.

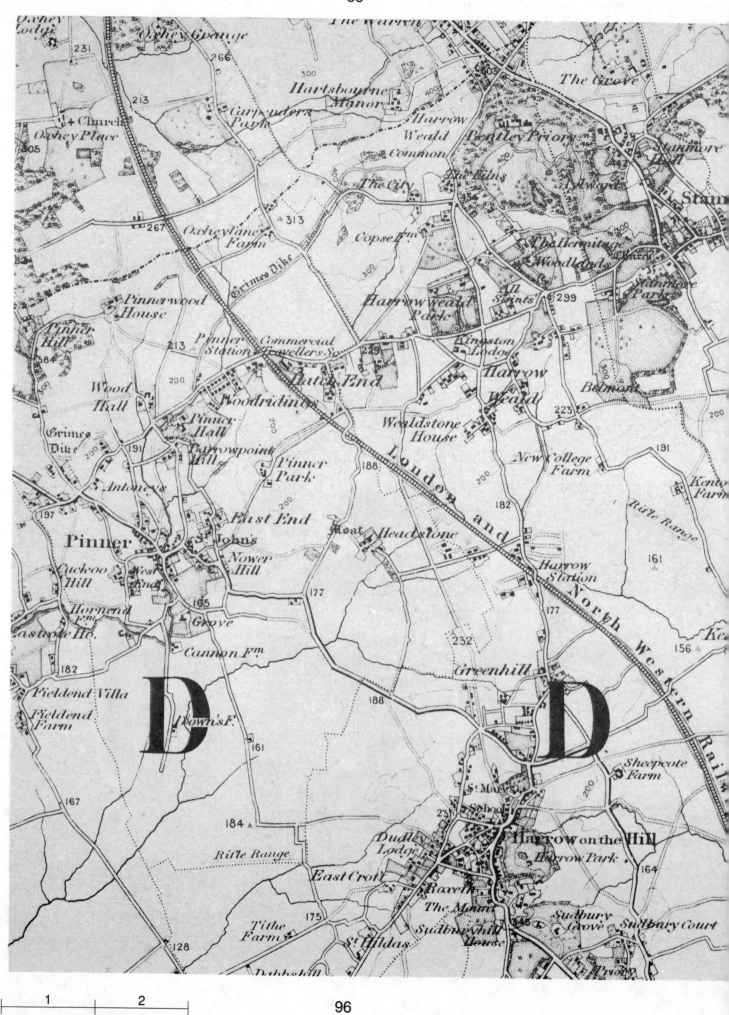

◁ 61

1   2

1 mile approx.

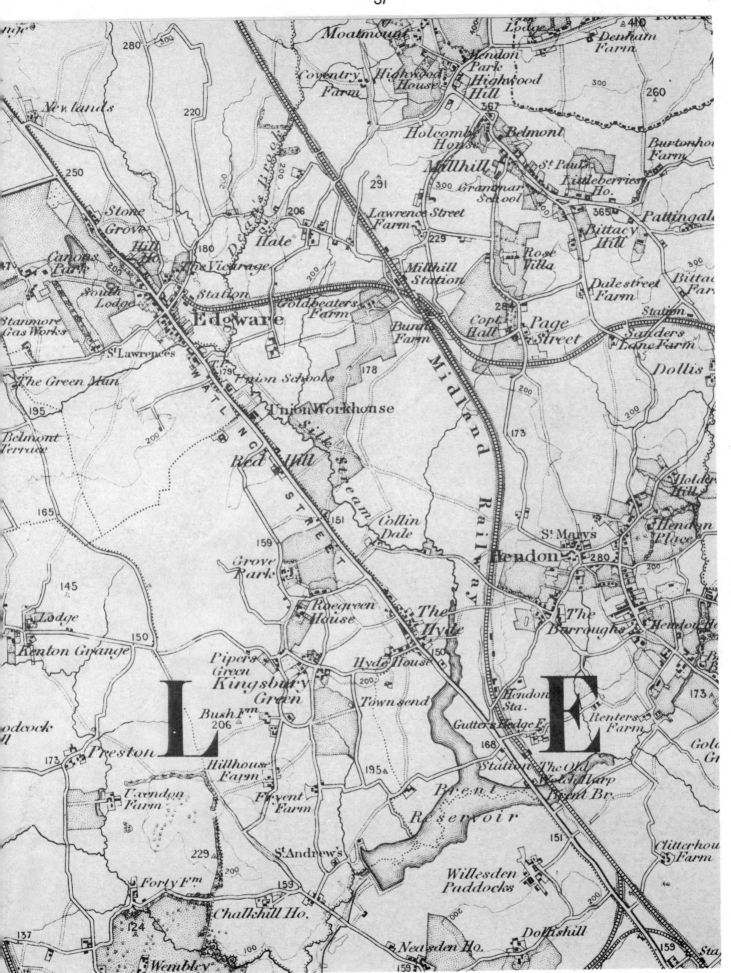

72 ▷

Surveyed 1862-1871. Published 1877.

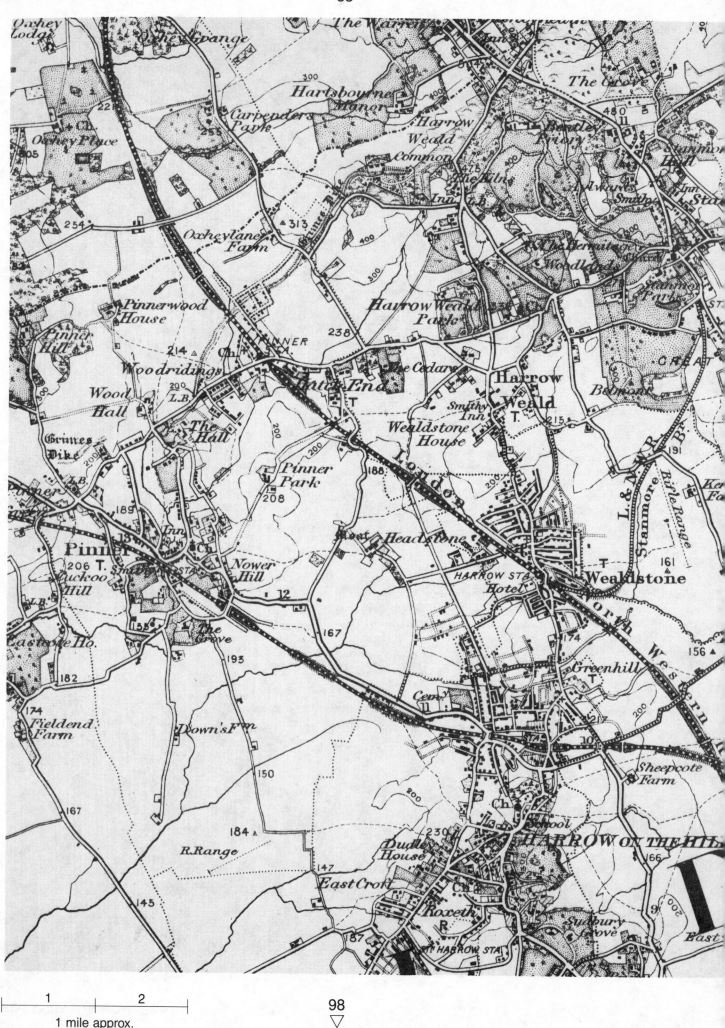

1 mile approx.

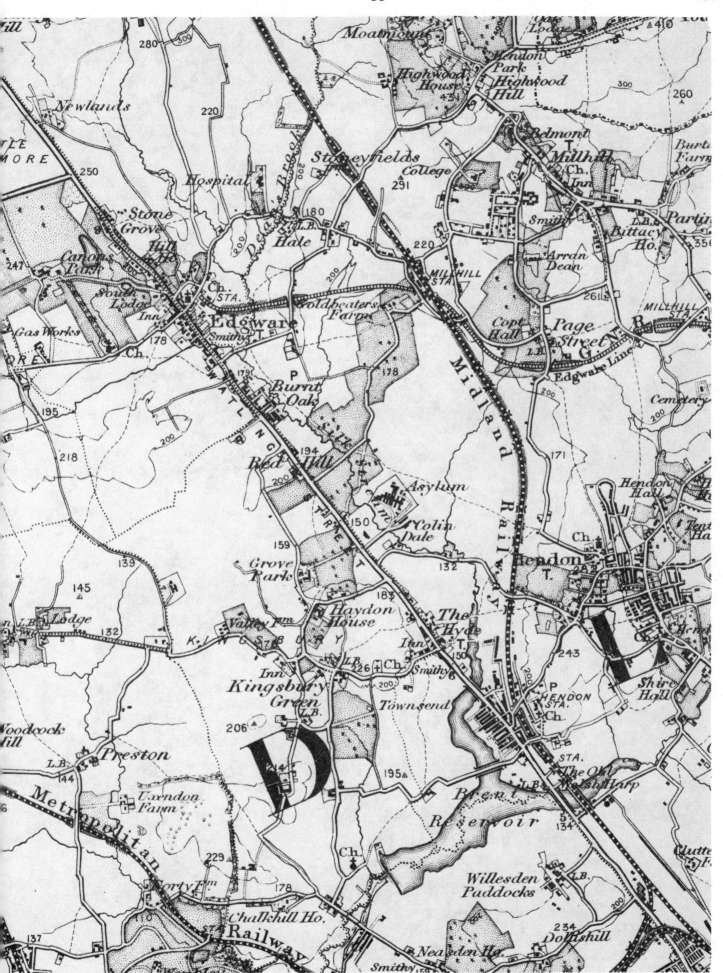

74 ▷

Surveyed 1862-1871. Revised 1902. Published 1904.

Burton
Hole

Brayers
Hill

Frith Manor

Moss Hall

Ervern
Burnet

Cobley Hatch
Wood
Ho.

aunders
ne

Nether
Street

Finchley

Dollis

Goals F.

Common

Finchley

Brown's
Wells

Coppis
F.

Tottenham Wood
F.

Nu

Holders Hill

Manor
House

East
End

Hog

Muswell
Hill

Decoy

Dirt House

Abbots F.

S

Bishops
Wood

Golders
Green

Caen Wood

Highgate

Horney
Lane

North End

Hampstead
Heath

Upper
Ho

Chatterhouse
F.

Childs
Hill

Millfield
F.

Mains
E.

Hampstead

The Slade

Pond Street

Toll bar

Kentish

76 ▷

Published 1822.

1   2

1 mile approx.

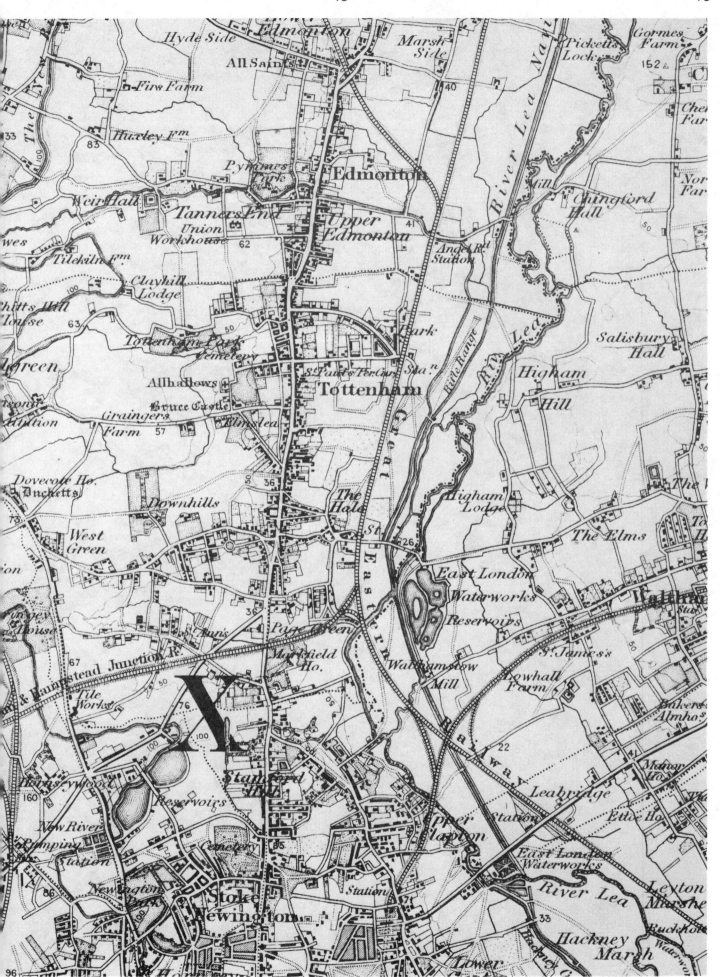

Surveyed 1862-1871. Published 1877.

◁ 69

1   2

1 mile approx.

80 ▷

Surveyed 1863-1876. Revised 1902. Published 1904.

1   2

1 mile approx.

Published 1805.

CHIG

White Hall

The Plâis
Fridayhill

ingford
Chingford Hatch

Larks Fm

mshire

Rolls

Chapel End

St John's

Finns

ver
mlet

Belmont Park
St Marys

Newbarns
Brookhouse

Lords Bushes

Woodford Wells

Monkham Fm

Luxborough

West Hatch

Broom Hill
Sweeps' Hill

Hill Ho.

Mount Pleasant

Higham's

Station

Hale End

Hall

Bellevue House

Woodford Green
Hart Ho.

Station

WOODFORD

Woodford
St Marys

Monkhams Ho.

Alnhurst

Rookery

Hill Farm

Woodford Bridge

St Pauls

Reading Ro.

The Parsonage

Claybury Hall

Claybury Park

Dumspring

Mossford Green
Trinity

Gryshamhall

Little Gearies

Sta

Hall

Grammar School

Stat

Forest Fo.

Knott's Green

Forest House

Hermon Hill

Clavhall

Carswell

Fernhall

Redbridge Cottage

esbrook

Wanstead

New Road

Hedgemans

The Rectory

Stonehall Farm

Highland F.

Valentine

Leyton Street

St John's

Walnut Tree Ho.

LowLeyton

Grove Fm

Deer Hall

Lake Ho.

Leyspring

WANSTEAD
Blake Hall
St Marys

Wanstead Park

Lincoln Island

The Temple

Cranbrook Park

South P

Ilford Lodge

City of London Cemetery

Ilford Cottage
Station

Leyton Park

Station

St Patrick's Cemetery

Holloway Down

Union Workhouse

Cann Hall

Wanstead Flats

Forest Gate

Wood Ho.

Hope Cottage

Manor Ho.

West Ham Hall

LITTLE ILFORD

Ilford Gaol

Gr
Ilf
B

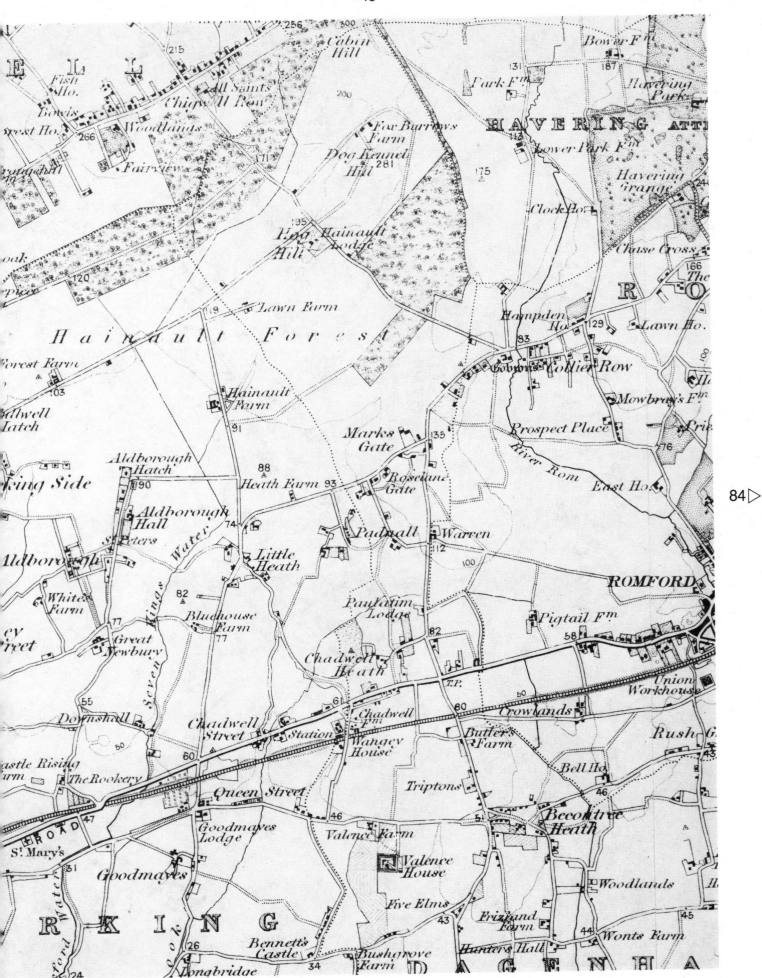

Surveyed 1862-1873. Published 1883.

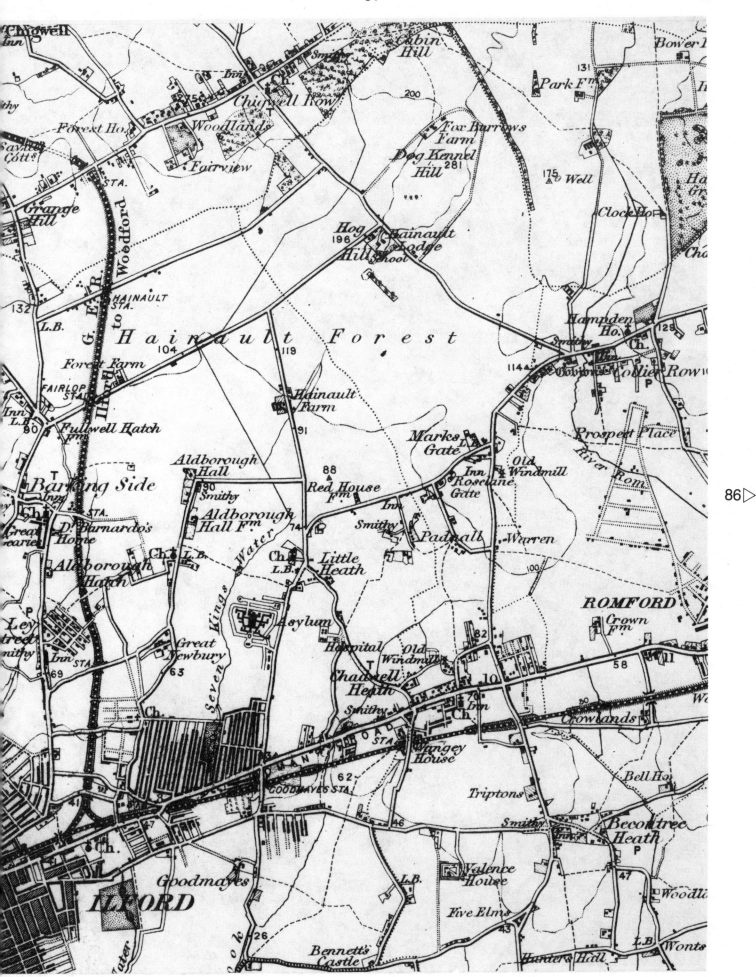

Surveyed 1862-1873. Revised 1903. Published 1904.

◁77

1   2

1 mile approx.

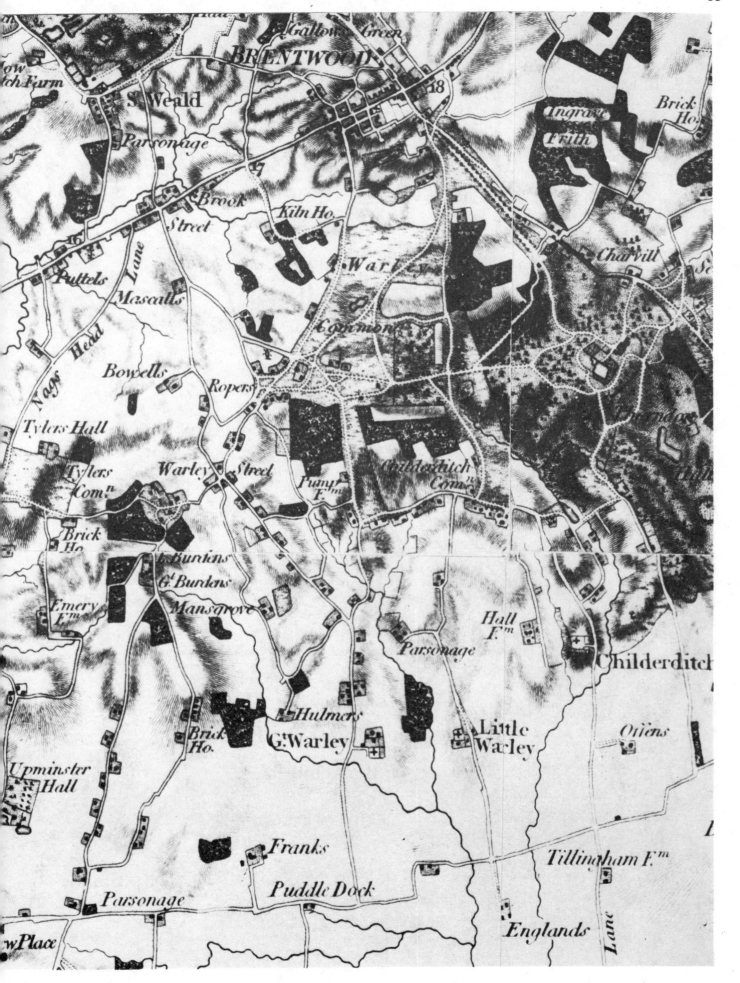

Published 1805.

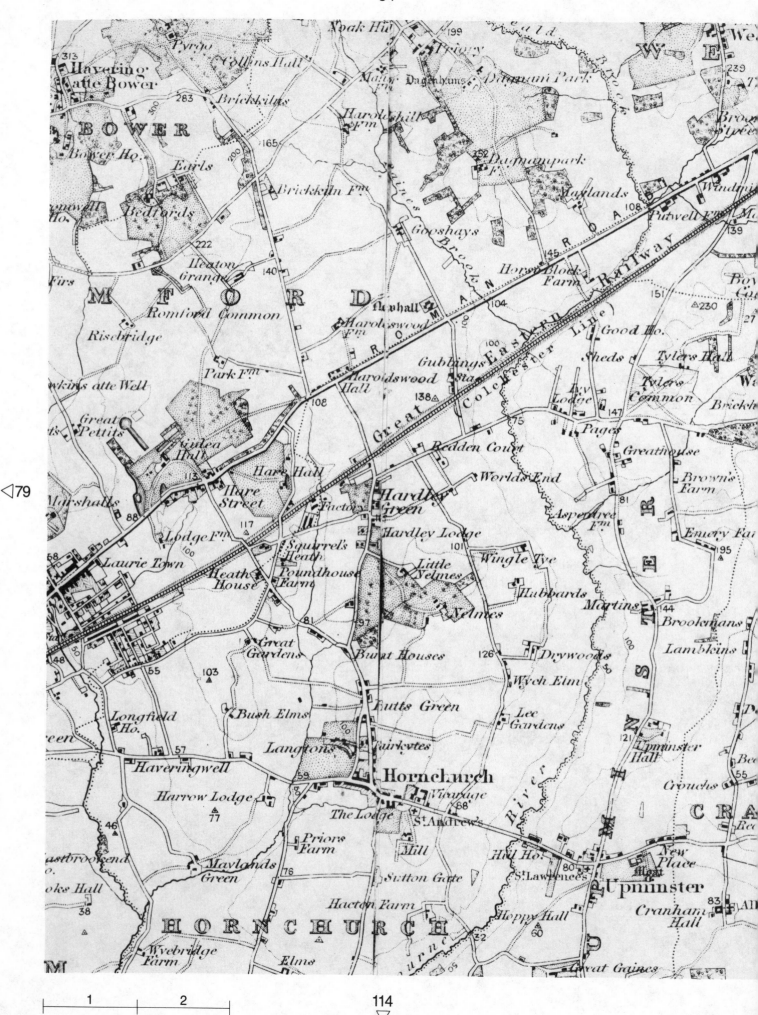

1 mile approx.

1   2

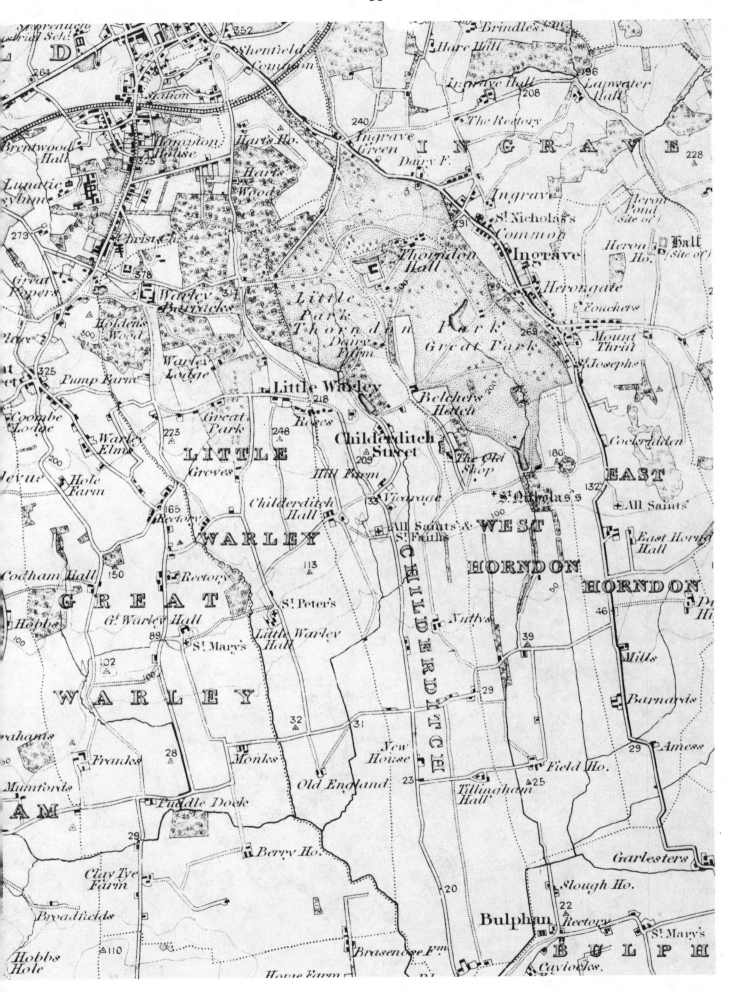

Surveyed 1862-1873. Published 1883.

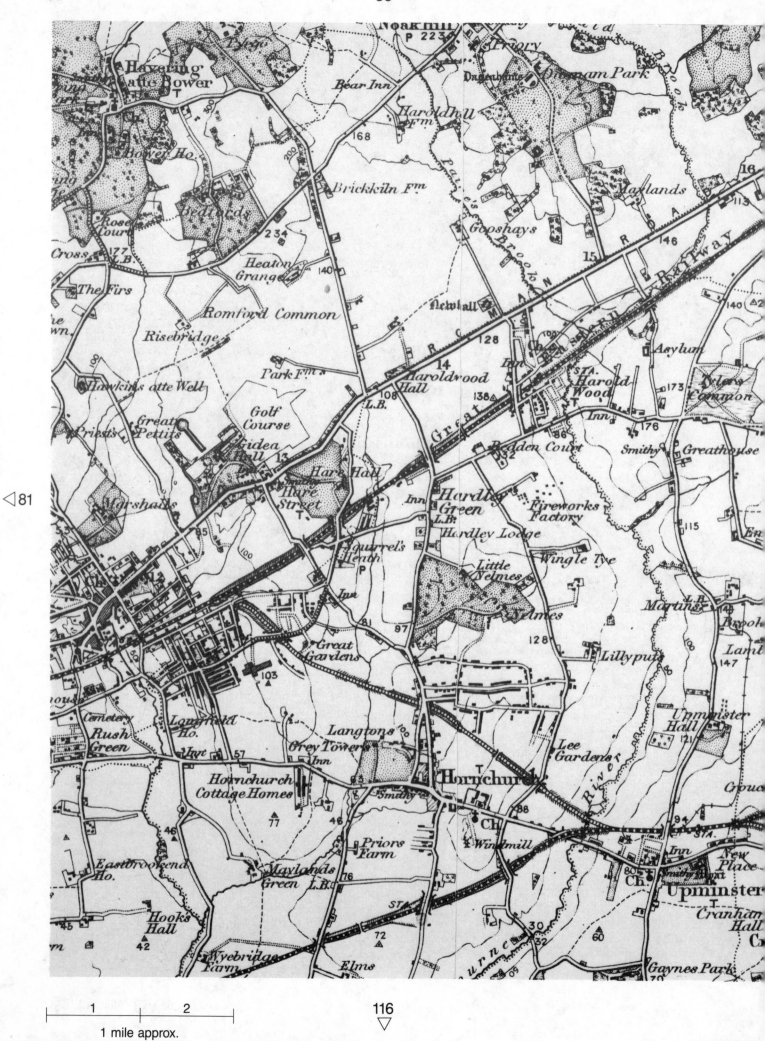

1 mile approx.

Surveyed 1862-1873. Revised 1903. Published 1904.

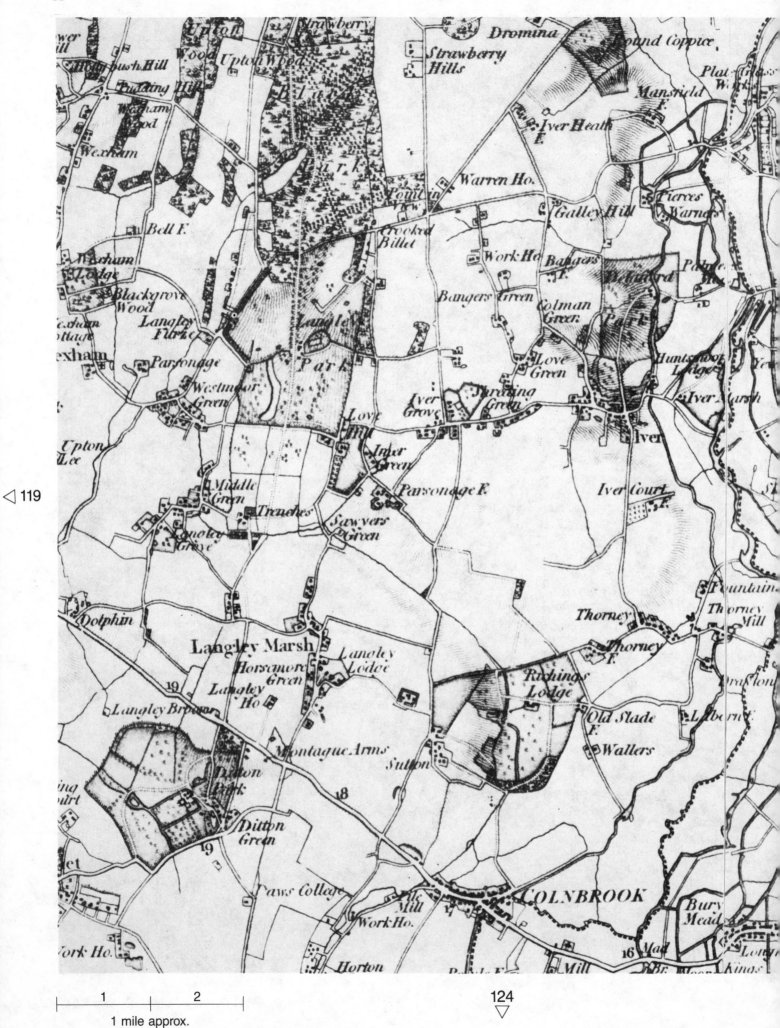

◁ 119

Upton
Wood Upton Wood

Strawberry

Dromina

ound Coppice

Strawberry
Hills

Plat Glass
Work

wer
ill

Menybush Hill

Mansfield
F.

Pudding Hill

Iver Heath

Wexham
Wood

B l a c k

Wexham

Warren Ho.

Pierces
Warners

P r k

Fountain
View

Galley Hill

Bell F.

Crooked
Billet

Work Ho

Bangers
F.

Deiford

Wexham
Lodge

Bangers Green

Colman
Green.

Park

Blackgrove
Wood

Langley
Furze

Langle

Wexham
ottage

Parsonage

Park

Love
Green

Huntsmoor
Lodge

Iver Marsh

exham

Westmoor
Green

Iver
Grove

reding
Green

Iver

Upton
Lee

Love
Hill

Iver
Green

Middle
Green

Parsonage F.

Iver Court

Trenches

Langley
Greve

Sawyers
Green

Fountain

Thorney

Thorney
Mill

Dolphin

Thorney
F.

Langley Marsh

Langley
Lodge

Richings
Lodge

Horsemore
Green

19

Old Slade
F.

Langley
Ho.

Colborn

Langley Brown

Montague Arms

Wallers

Ditton
Park

Sutton

18

ing
ourt

Ditton
Green

9

aws College

de
Mill

COLNBROOK

Bury
Mead

Work Ho.

Work Ho.

Horton

Mill

16

Mill

Kings

1   2

1 mile approx.

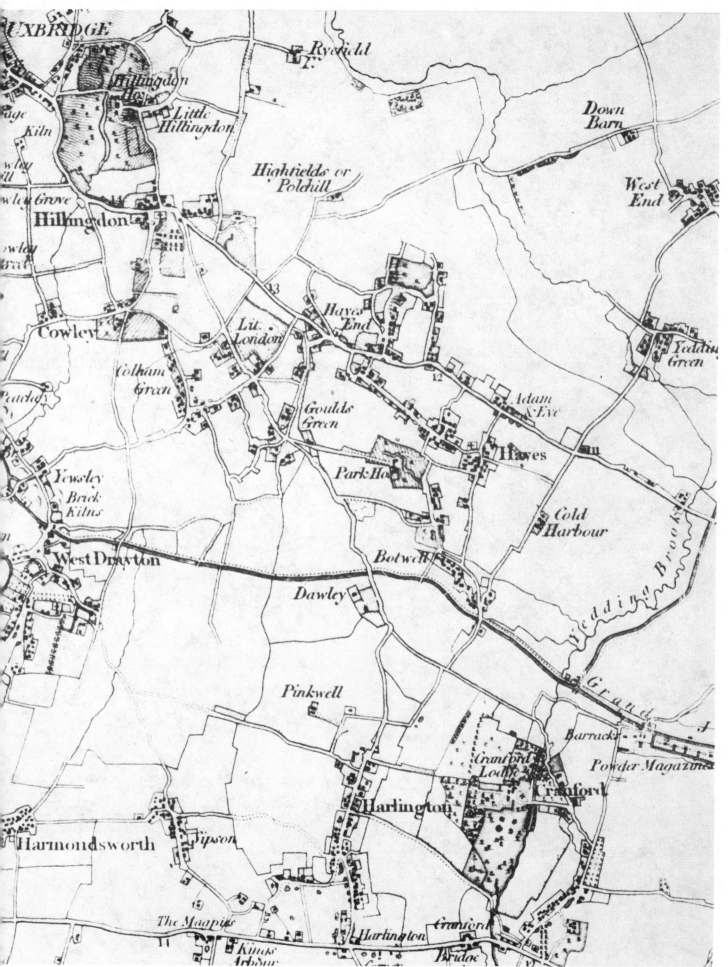

Published 1816-1822.

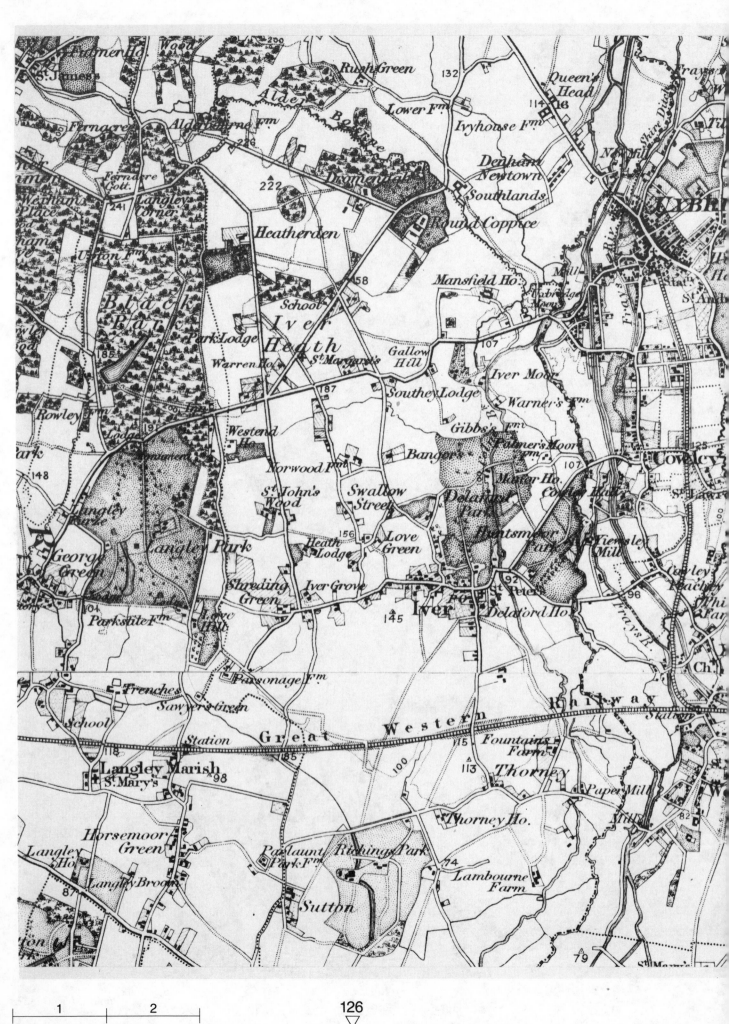

1 mile approx.

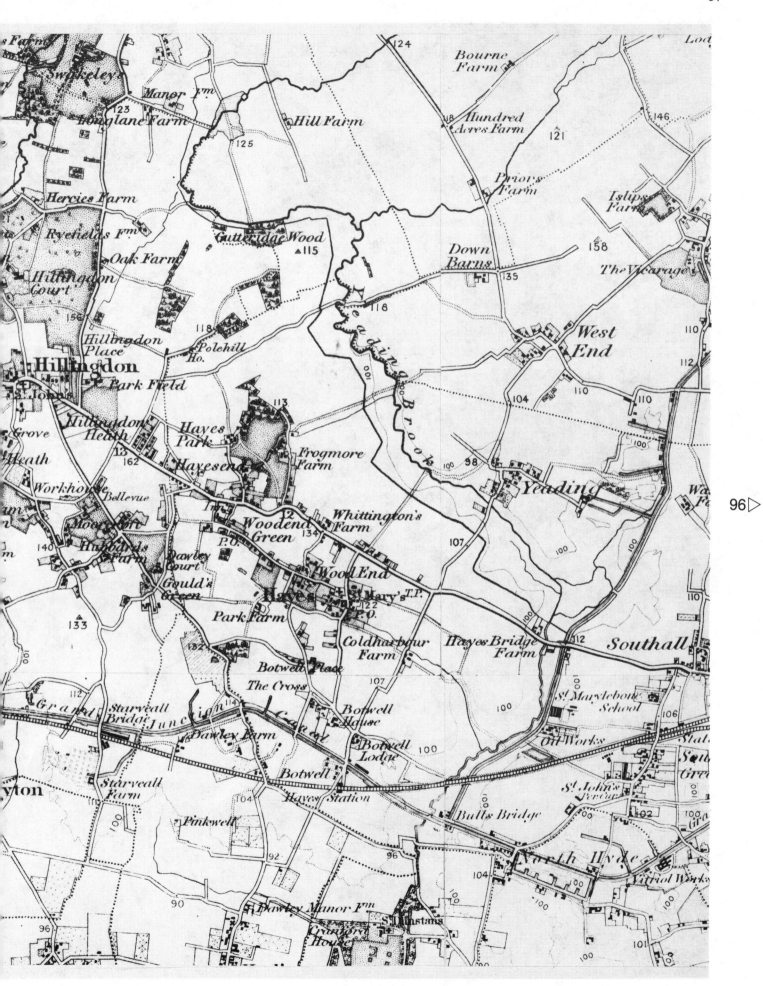

Surveyed 1863-1876. Published 1880.

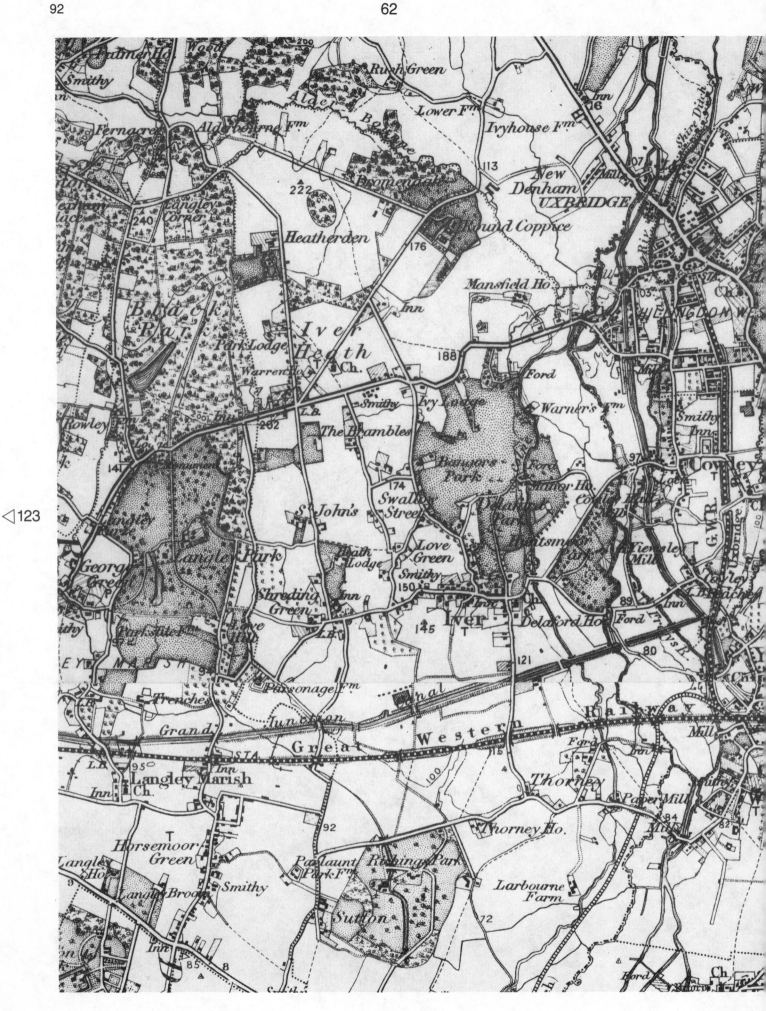

◁123

1   2

1 mile approx.

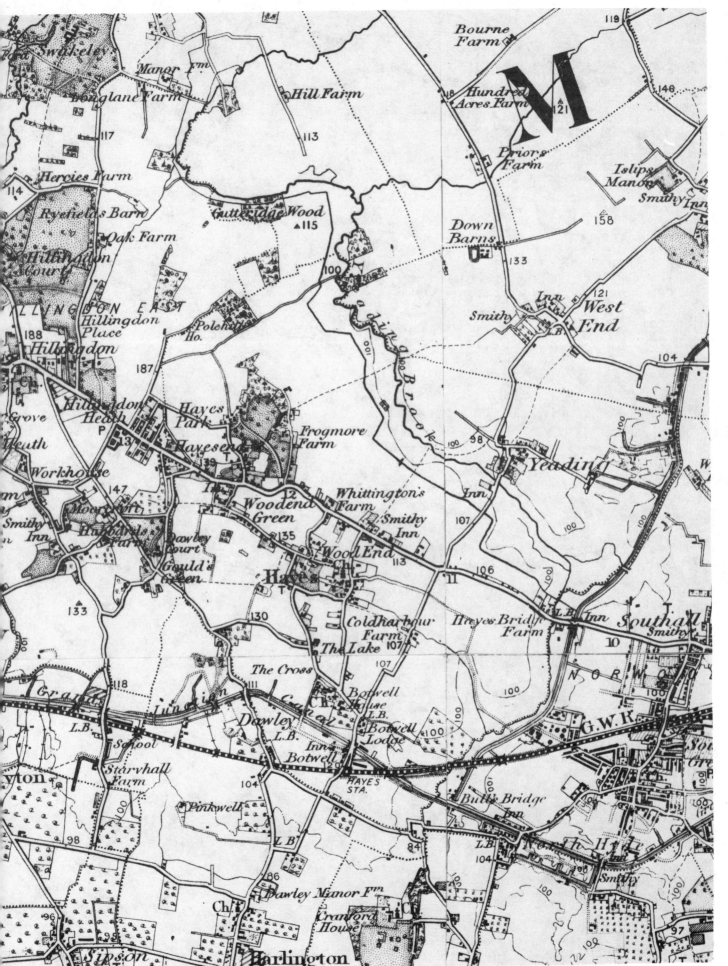

Surveyed 1863-1876. Revised 1902. Published 1904.

Horsington
Wood

Horsington
Green

Ilus
Green

Northolt

Court

Paddington Canal

Parsonage

Perivale

Greenford

Manor

Brent River

Brentside

Pitch-hanger

Castle Hill

Lodge

Wœdey

Castle Bear
Hill

Drayton
Green

Hanwell
Park

Swing
Bridge

Dormans
Wells

Sluice

Mill

Southall

Old Hats

Dean

10

Hanwell

Ealing

9

Ealing

Southall
Park

Hanwell

Little
Ealing

Southall
Green

Heath

Canal

Boston
F.

Drum
Lane

nction
Norwood

Menagerie

North
Hyde

Osterly

Boston
Ho.

Park

Wick
Green

Sion Hill

Heston
Ho.

Heston

BRENTFORD

Brick
Kilns

Sutton

1   2

1 mile approx.

Published 1822.

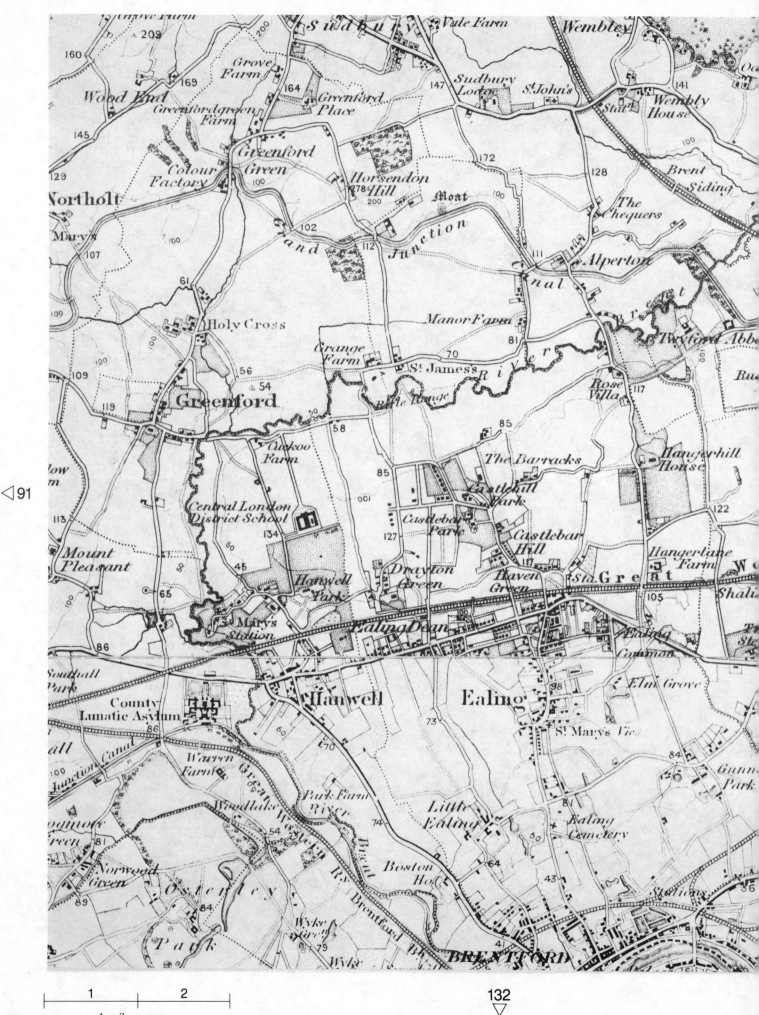

91

1   2

1 mile approx.

102 ▷

Surveyed 1861-1871. Published 1876-77.

1   2

1 mile approx.

104 ▷

Surveyed 1861-1871. Revised 1901-1902. Published 1904.

West
End

Rosslyn
Ho.

Town

Chapel

Haverstock
Hill

Spring
Place

Copenhagen
Ho.

Balsize
Ho.

Chalcott

Chalk F.

Islin

Primrose
Hill

Camden
Town

Portland
Town

Barr
acks

St Pancras

Pentonville

REGENTS
PARK

Somers
Town

Kilburn Wells

ilburn

Maida

Paddington

Westbourn
Green

Grd Junction
Water Works

Reservoir

HYDE
PARK

Craven
Place Bayswater

ngton
el Pits

Gardens

Serpentine River

GREEN
PARK

JAMES

Palace

Kensington

Westmin
ster Br

Waterloo
Bridge

Grove

Brompton

Knights
Bridge

Work
Ho.

Earls Terrace

Pavilion

Pavilion

Penitentiary

Earls
Court

Old
Brompton

Queens Elm

Lambeth

Little
Chelsea

Hospital

Mill Bank Bridge

Vauxhall
Gard

Walham
Green

Chelsea

M

Red Ho.
Regens

E

Vine
Elm

Lambeth

106 ▷

Published 1822.

◁ 97

1   2

1 mile approx.

Surveyed 1861-1868. Published 1876.

◁ 99

△
74

140
▽

1 mile approx.

75

105

110 ▷

Greenwich
Marshes

Surveyed 1861-1871. Revised 1902. Published 1904.

1   2

1 mile approx.

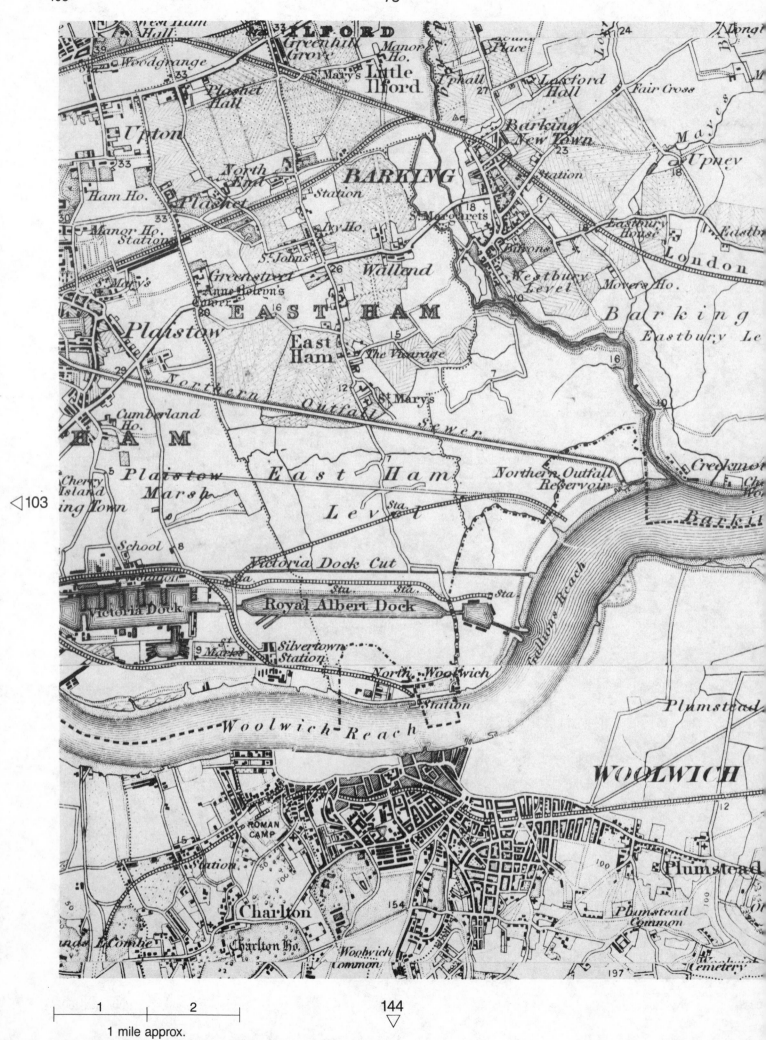

◁103

1   2

1 mile approx.

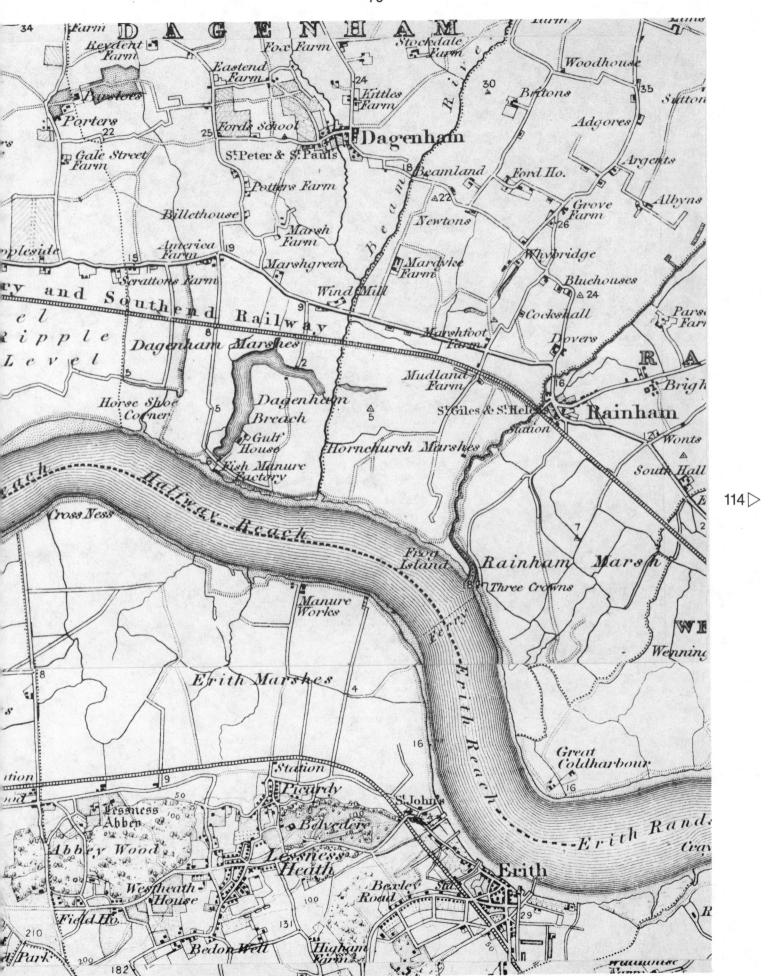

Surveyed 1862-1873. Published 1888.

105

146

1 mile approx.

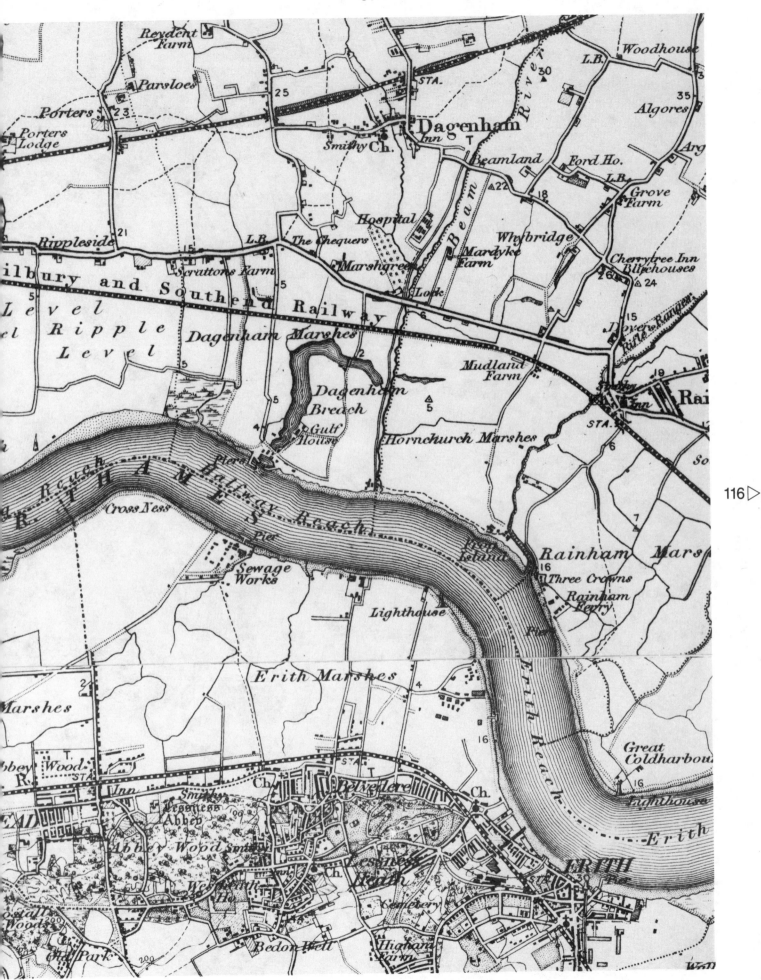

Surveyed 1862-1873. Revised 1903. Published 1904.

◁107

1   2

1 mile approx.

Published 1805.

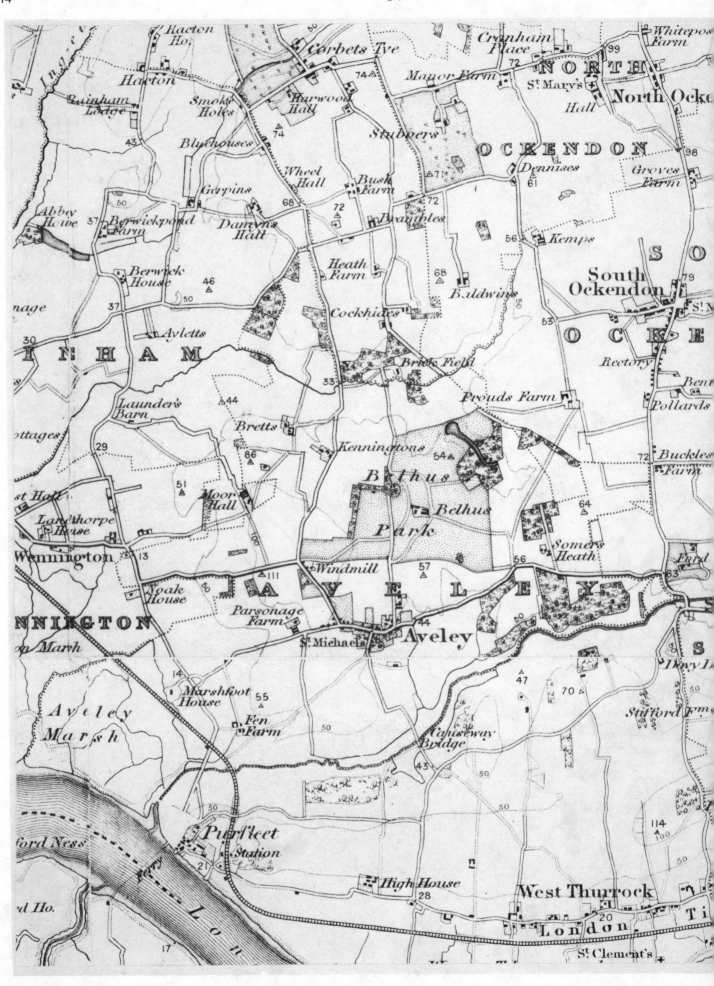

◁109

150
▽

1 | 2
1 mile approx.

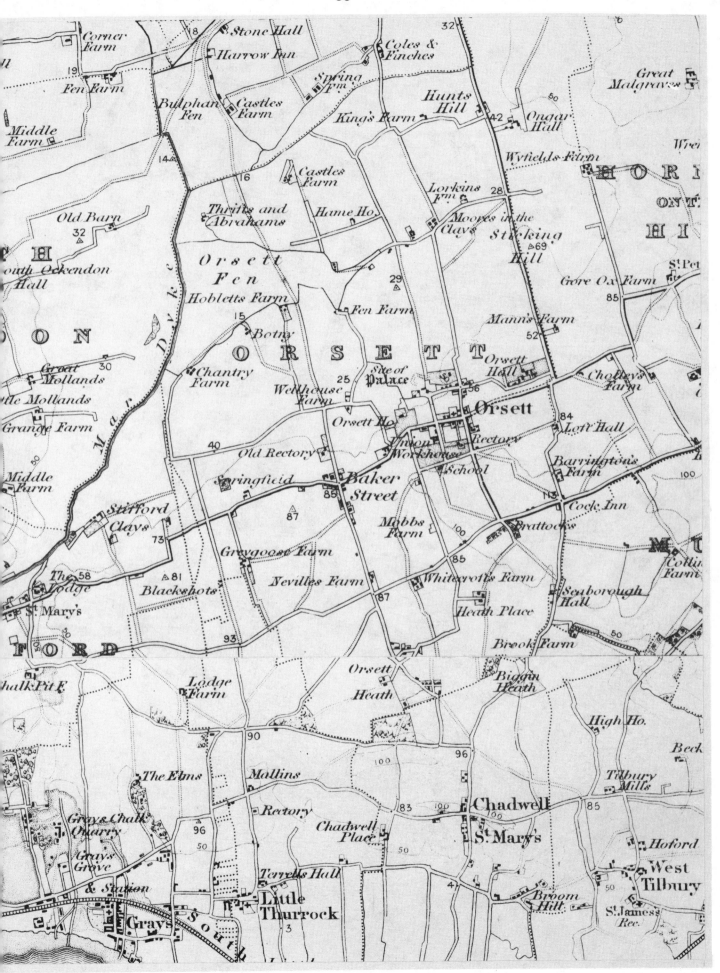

Surveyed 1862-1873. Published 1883.

111

1   1   2

1 mile approx.

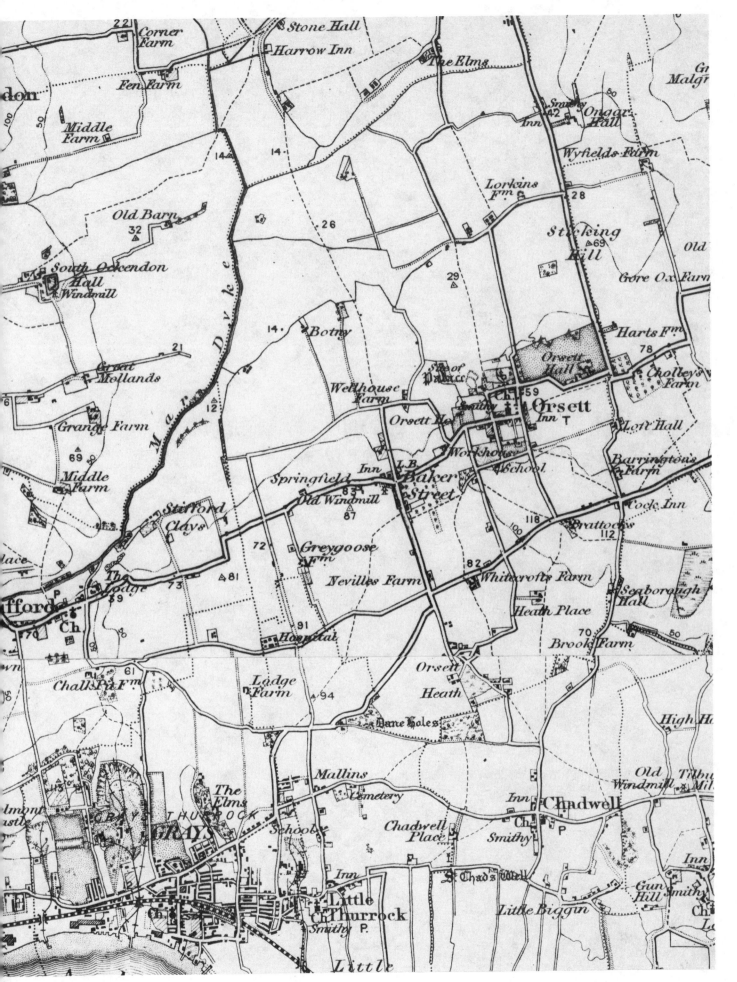

Surveyed 1862-1873. Revised 1903. Published 1904.

1 mile approx.

88/124 ▷

Published 1816.

Nordon Fm | Boyne Villa | Row | 110 | 107 | Staverton Lodge | West Town Farm | 79 | Barge Farm | 74 | Amaiden Ho. | Shoppenhangers Fm | St Michael's | Bray Wick | BRAY | Jesus Hospital | 72 | Monkey Is. | St. James's | Fox Green | Kimber's Ho. | 90 | Canon Hill | 87 | Ockwells | 86 | Elm Lodge | Queen's Eyot | Builder's Well | 80 | Down Place | Oakley Court | Moat Fm | Philberd's Fm | 86 | Philberds | Holyport | Stroud Farm | Stud Green | 96 | 100 | Bartlett's Ho. | Foxley's Farm | Foxley's | Moneyrow Green | Fifield Lodge | Paley Street | Boading Fm | 120 | Church | 97 | Fifield | Bishop's Farm | Oakley Place | Touchen end | Ledger Farm | Fifield Ho. | School | 106 | 102 | Oakley | Mount Scipett Farm | Haweshill | All Saints | Vicarage | 127 | 118 | New Lodge Fm | 131 | Windsor | Pickford's Fm | Park Farm | New Lodge | 219 | Forest | 149 | Redstone Farm | Braywood Fm | Foliejon Park | 200 | Critchfield Ho. | 194 | 238 | Hawthorn Hill | 250 | 200 | 233 | Winkfield | Nuptown | Chawridge Manor Fm | 240 | Dairy Farm | 230 | 207 | Jealotts Hill | 200 | 225 | Crouchlane Farm | Row | 245 | Malthill Farm | 241 | Winkfield Street | North Lodge | 250 | St. Michael & | St. Mary's | Ascot Cottage | St. Peter's

1 | 2

1 mile approx.

90/126 ▷

Surveyed 1874. Published 1880.

1 mile approx.

92/128▷

Surveyed 1863-1874. Revised 1901-1902. Published 1904.

thley Ho.
thley
Rectory
Berkin
Poyle
Horton
Mills
Hortons
Horton
Ho.
reneek
Willyhouse
Moor F.
Upper Mill
Corn Mill
Place F.
Copper
Mills
Powder Mills
Stanwell
Moor
Place
Barn
Stanw
Place
Ferry
Priory
Cottage
Wharf
Wyrardisbury
Staines Moor
F.
River
Little
Ankerwyke
Magna
Charta
Island
Ho.
Staines
Priest
Hill
Long
Mead
Gr.t Ankerwyke
Hythe
End
Moor
Yoveney
Hammonds
T. Pike
nkerwyke
Runney
Mead
London
Stone
Duncroft
Ho.
STAINES
wood
Ode
Knowles
Ge.
Shortwood
Com.
18
17
T.P.
Egham
Vicarage
Withygate
Field
gham
Hill
Hith
Egham
19
Lit. Foster
Ho.
Thorpe
Lee
Rusham
Green
ham
Ho.
Rusham
House
Thorpe
Foster
House
Leddingt.n
Ho.
Field
Whit
Hill
Gallow
Stroud
Green
Penton
Hook
Thorpe
La
Ferry

1   2

1 mile approx.

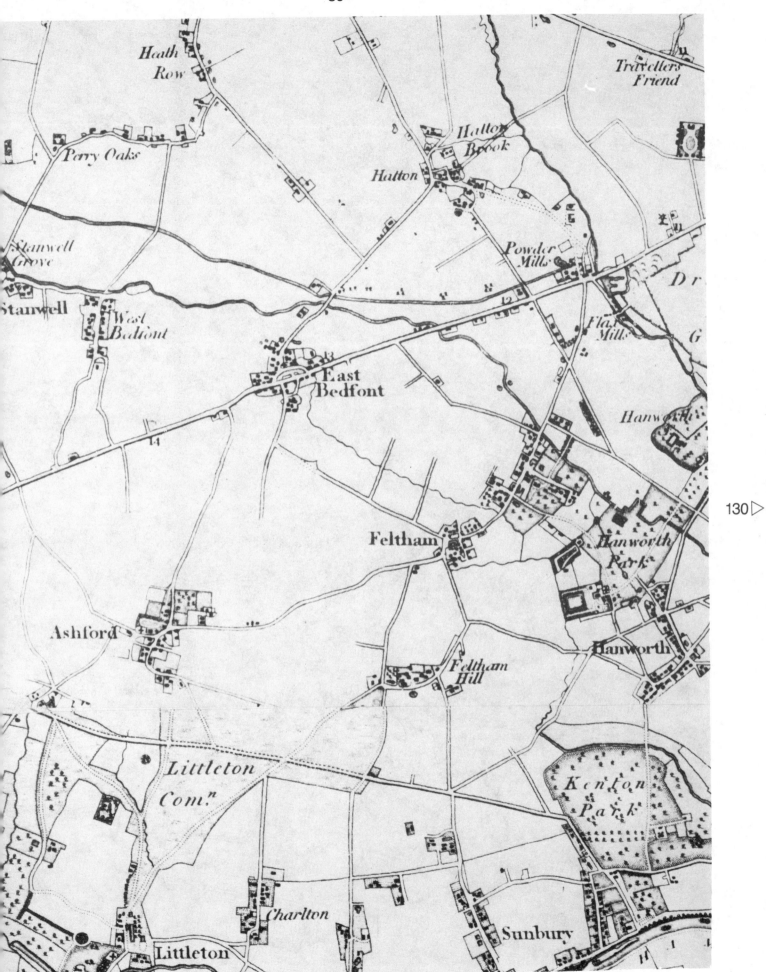

Published 1822.

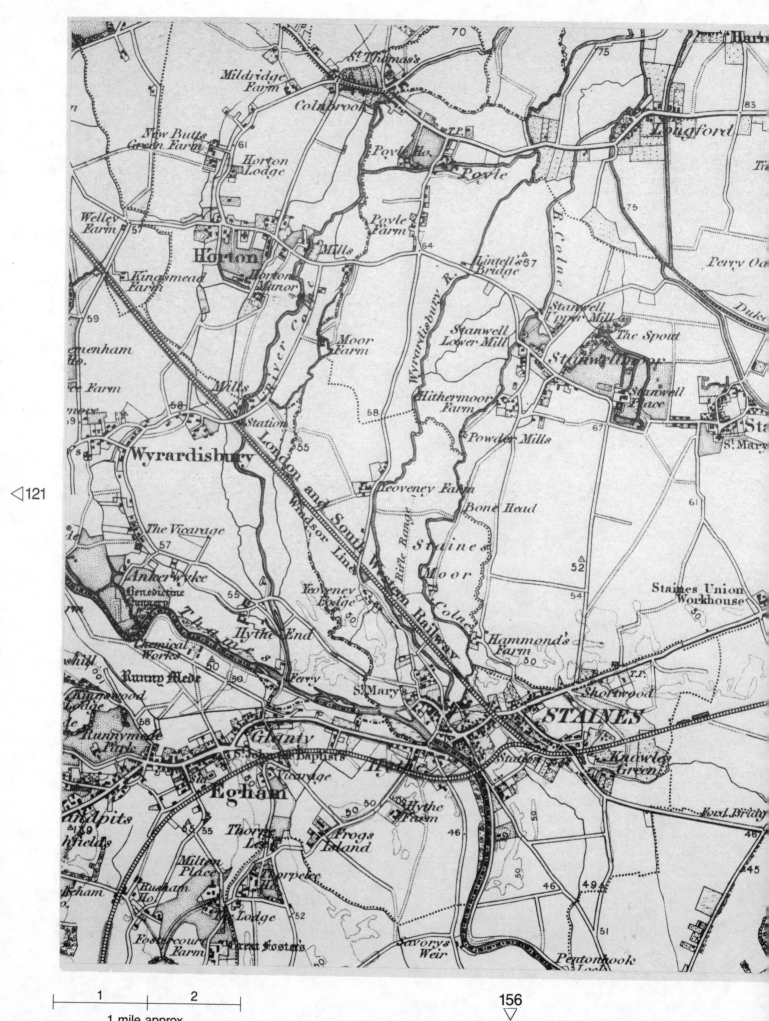

70

75

St Thomas's

Mildridge
Farm

Colnbrook

T.P.

83

Longford

New Butts
Green Farm

61

Povle Ho.

Povle

Horton
Lodge

Welley
Farm

57

Povle
Farm

Mills

64

Lintell's
Bridge

67

Perry Oa

Horton

Kingsmead
Farm

Horton
Manor

R. Colne

Duke

Moor
Farm

Stanwell
Upper Mill

The Spout

59

Stanwell
Lower Mill

Stanwell Moor

menham

Farm

Mills

58

58

Hithermoor
Farm

Stanwell
Place

Station

55

Powder Mills

St

St Mary

Wyraraisbury R.

London and South Western Railway

Wyrardisbury

121

Heoveney Farm

Bone Head

61

The Vicarage

57

Staines
Moor

52

Anterwyke

Windsor Line

Rifle Range

R. Colne

54

Staines Union
Workhouse

Benedictine

55

Yeoveney
Lodge

50

50

Hythe End

Chemical
Works

50

Hammond's
Farm

50

Runny Mede

50

Ferry

St Mary

T.P.

Shortwood

STAINES

Kingswood
Lodge

58

Runnymede
Park

Egham

Egianty

St John the Bapust's

Vicarage

Hythe

Station

Knowles
Green

alpits

hields

55

55

Thorpe
Lea

Frogs
Island

Hythe
Farm

50

46

Ford Bridg

46

Milton
Place

orpe

50

49

45

Rusham
Ho.

Lodge

52

50

46

49

51

Fostscourt
Farm

Great Fosters

Savorys
Weir

Pentonhook
Lock

1   2

1 mile approx.

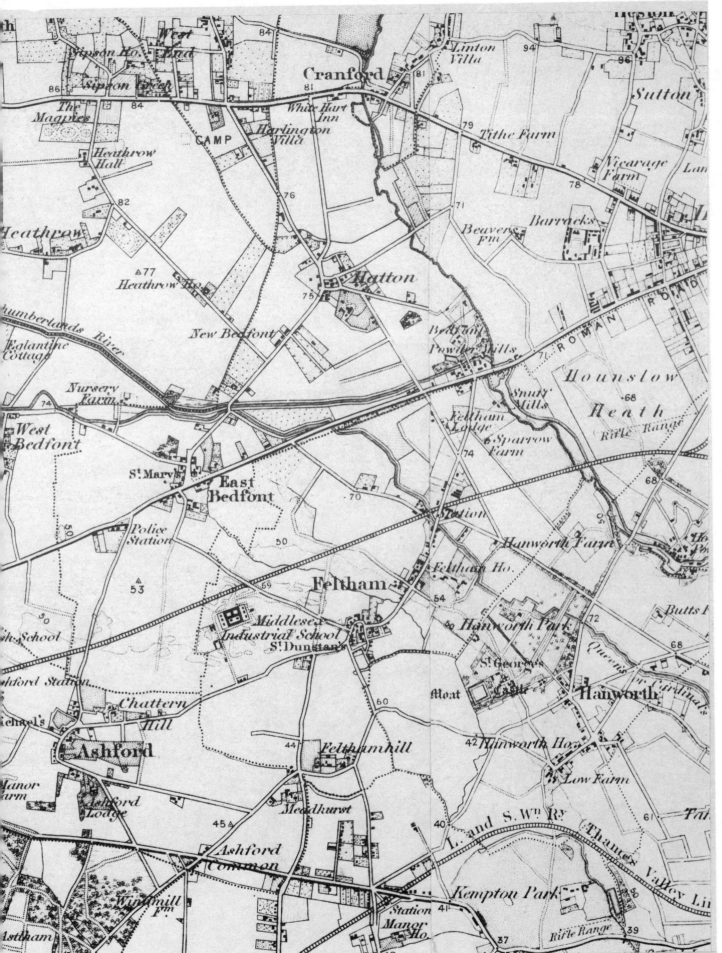

Surveyed 1874. Published 1880.

◁123

1 mile approx.

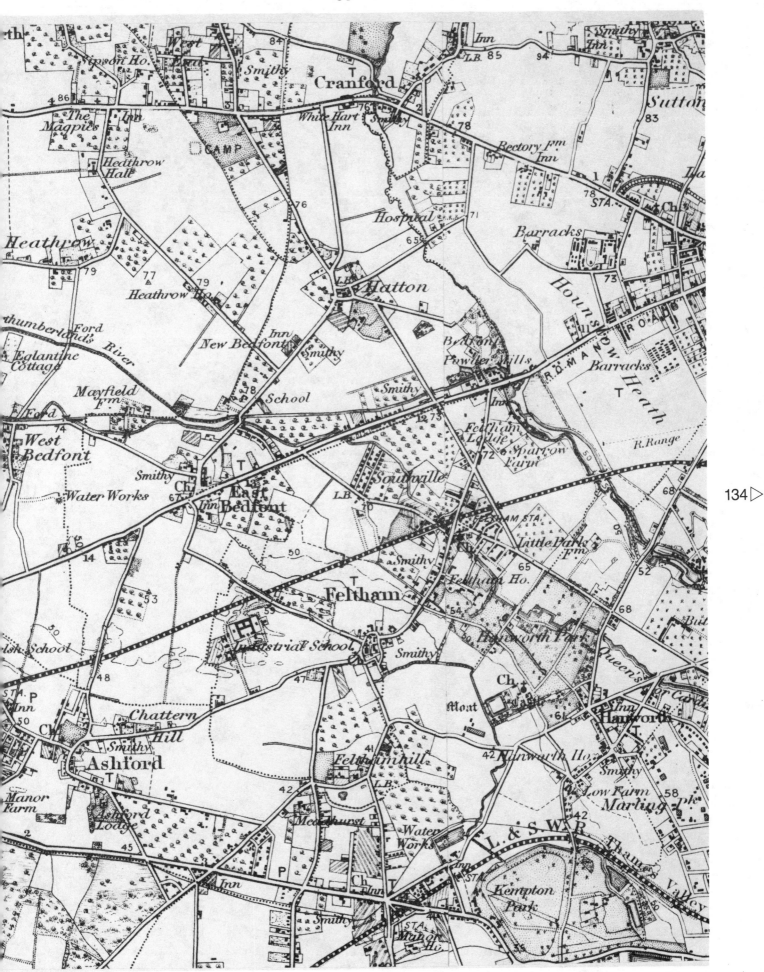

134 ▷

Surveyed 1863-1874. Revised 1901-1902. Published 1904.

1   2

1 mile approx.

136 ▷

Published 1816.

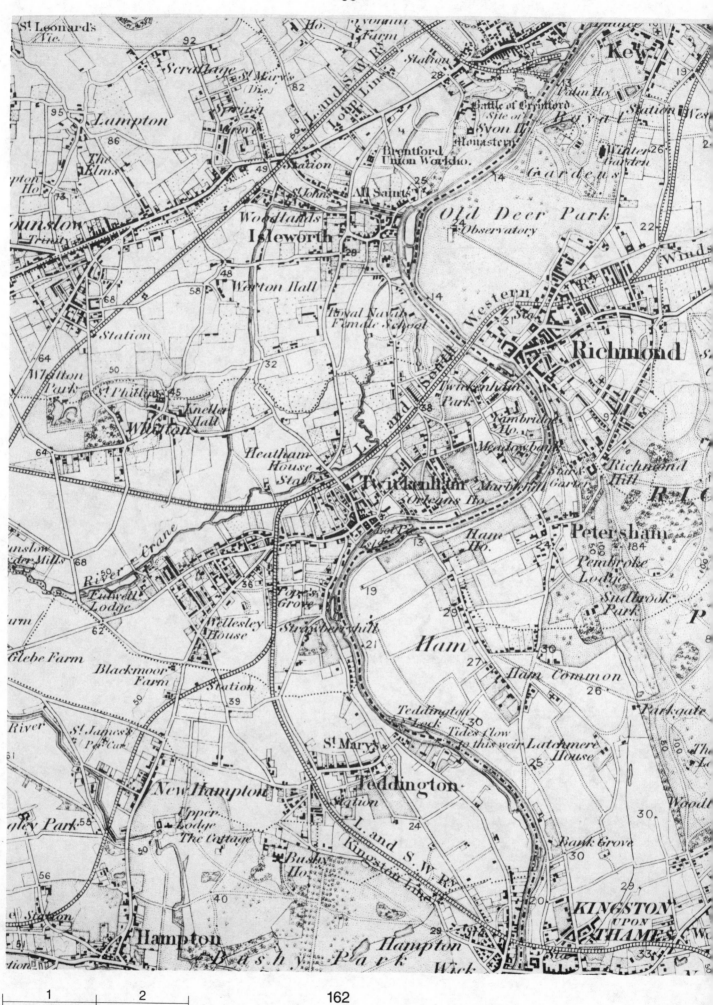

◁127

1   2

1 mile approx.

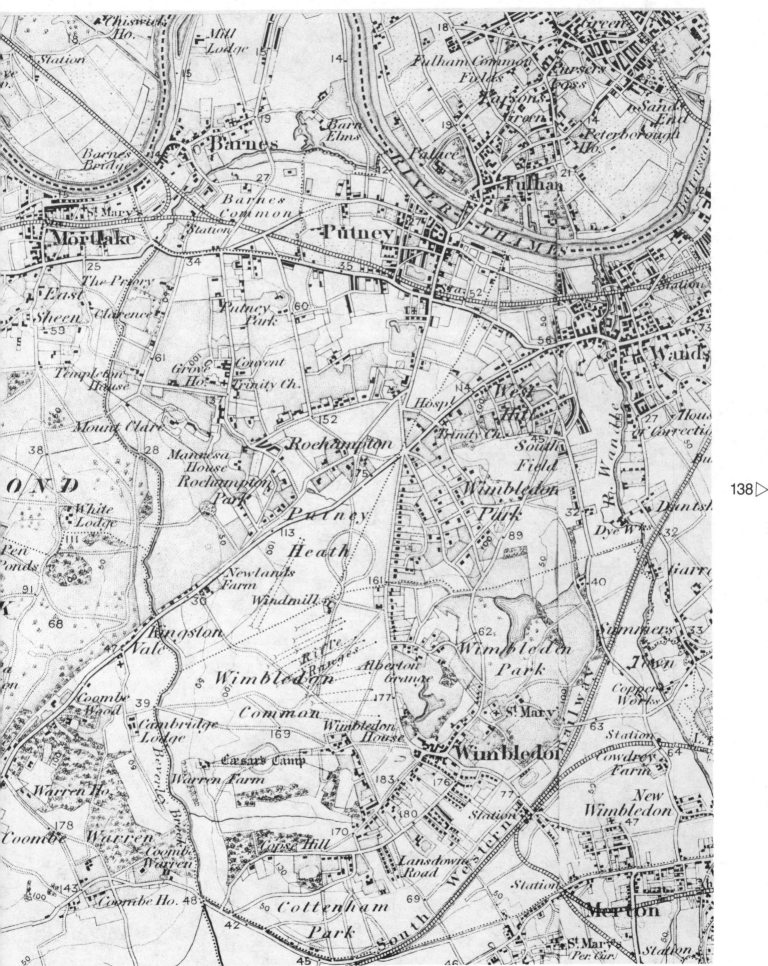

Surveyed 1861-1871. Published 1876.

◁ 129

1   2

1 mile approx.

140 ▷

Surveyed 1861-1871. Revised 1901-1902. Published 1904.

Parsons Green

Sandy End

Battersea

Battersea Fields

Battersea New Town

South Ville

Stockwell

Piddocs F.

York Br.

York Place

Battersea Rise

Clapham

Clapham Common

Wandsworth Common

Half Farthing

Bleak Hall

Brixton Causeway

Brixton Hill

Dunsford Ho.

Iron Railway

Balham Hill

Chapel

Hind F.

Garret Mill

Burntwood Lane

Upper Garret

Upper Tooting

Work Ho.

Common

Streatham

Garret Green

Cowdry F.

Tooting

Merton Mill

Colliers Wood

Streatham Com.

Wells

Princes Head

Graveney Bridge

Jacobs Green

Biggins F.

Plows Marsh

Merton Abbey

Phipps Bridge

Mitcham Wood

1   2

1 mile approx.

142 ▷

Published 1816.

◁ 133

1   2

1 mile approx.

144 ▷

Surveyed 1861-1871. Published 1876.

◁135

1   2

1 mile approx.

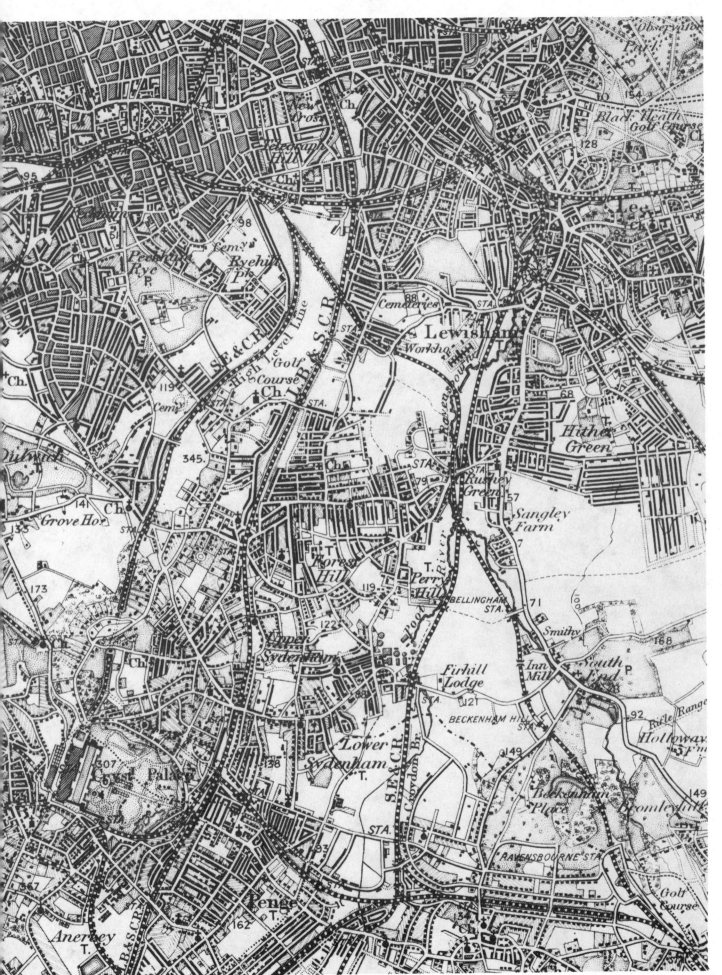

Surveyed 1861-1871. Revised 1901-1902. Published 1904.

Myrtle
Place

Black 6

Sun
in Sands

Lower
Kidbrook

Mordant
College

Upper
Kidbrook

Heath

Black
Heath

Shooters
Hill

Woolwich
Com.ᵗⁿ

Lee Church

Wricklesmarsh

Severndroog Castle

Well
Hall

Lee

Park
F.ᵐ

Eltham

Hither
Green

Horn
Park

Middle
Park

Pollet

Burnt Ash
Gr.

Southend

Burnt
Ash

Eltham
Place

ney

Mottingham

Pope Str

Whitechaple
Farm

Clay
Farm

Shrofield

Southend

Cold Harbor

Warren
Ho.

Sundridge

Elmsted

Belm

Prick

Plastow

Camden
Place

Grove

Camden
Common

BROMLEY

1   2

1 mile approx.

Published April 18th 1805.

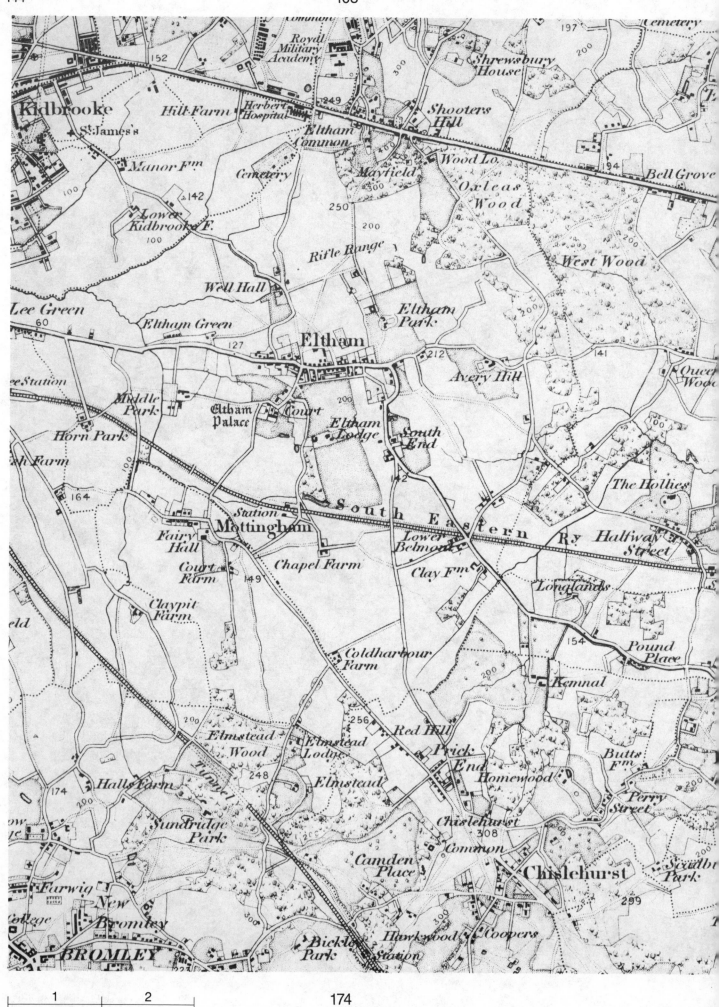

Kidbrooke
St James's
Hill Farm
Herbert Hospital
Royal Military Academy
Shrewsbury House
Shooters Hill
Wood Lo.
Manor F^m
Cemetery
Eltham Common
Mayfield
Oxleas Wood
Bell Grove
Lower Kidbrooke F.
Rifle Range
West Wood
Well Hall
Eltham Park
Lee Green
Eltham Green
Eltham
Avery Hill
Queen Wood
Lee Station
Middle Park
Eltham Court
Eltham Palace
Eltham Lodge
South End
The Hollies
Horn Park
Farm
Station
Mottingham
Fairy Hall
South Eastern Ry
Halfway Street
Lower Belmont
Court Farm
Chapel Farm
Clay F^m
Longlands
Claypit Farm
Pound Place
Kemnal
Coldharbour Farm
Elmstead Wood
Elmstead Lodge
Red Hill
Prick End
Homewood
Butts F^m
Elmstead
Perry Street
Halls Farm
Tunnel
Chislehurst
Common
Sundridge Park
Camden Place
Chislehurst
South Park
Farwig
New Bromley
College
BROMLEY
Bickley Park
Bickley Station
Hawkwood
Coopers

1   2
1 mile approx.

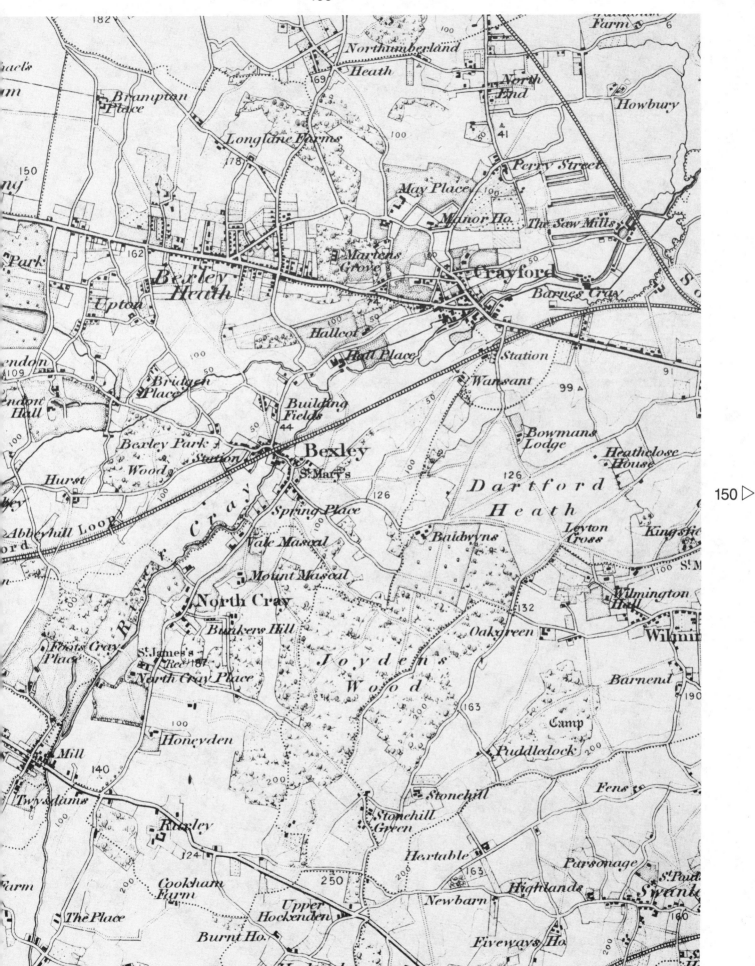

Surveyed 1861-1868. Published 1876.

1   2

1 mile approx.

Surveyed 1861-1868. Revised 1903. Published 1905.

△

◁143

1   2

1 mile approx.

West
Thurrock

Mill

DeVer Wharf

Grays
Hall

Chadwell Pla

Grays
Thurrock

Little Thurrock

MARSH

ST CLEMENTS REACH

NORTHFLEET HOPE

WEST TIL

MARSH

Greenhithe

Ingress

18

19

Galley Hill

Stone
Br.

The Hi

WEST

GRA

Knockholt

North
Fleet

Northfleet Hithe

Stone
Castle

Milton
Street

20

GRAVESE

Pell Street

Hockenden

Swanscomb

Parsonage

21

Swanscomb Park W.

Windfield Bank

Wombwell
Hall

Perry
Street

Stone
Wood

Telegraph

Bean

Bundle
F.

Betsham

South
Fleet

Sandbury

Green Street
Green

Hazle

Northfleet
Green

Hook
Place

Broad ditch

Westwood

Hook
Gr.

Red
Street

Published 1805.

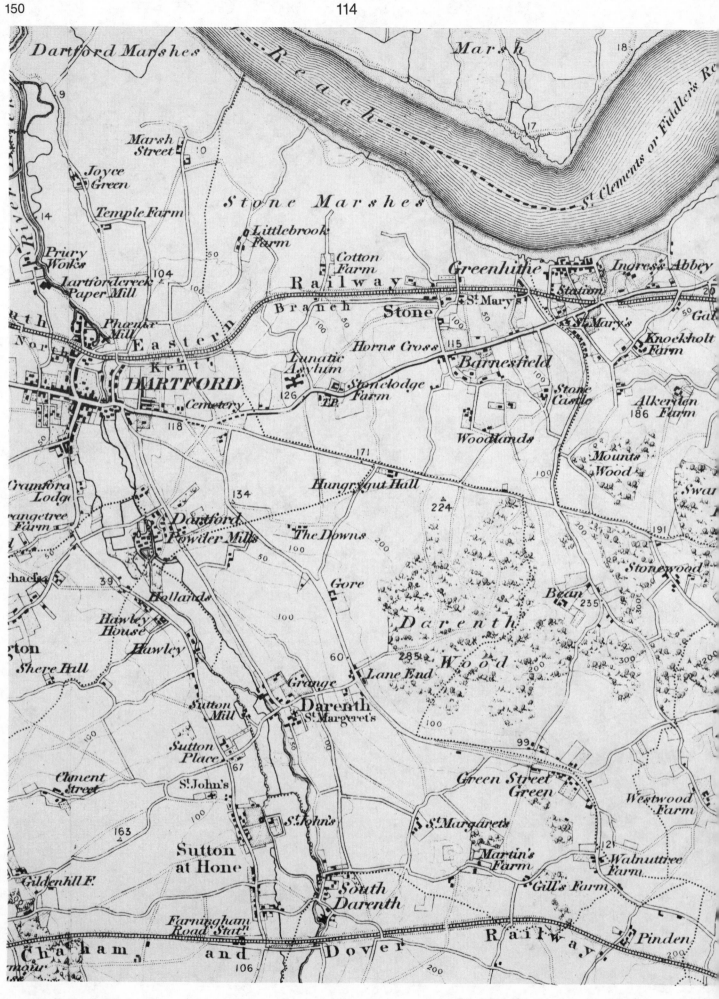

Dartford Marshes

Marsh

18

Reach

St Clements or Fiddler's Re

9

17

Marsh
Street

Joyce
Green

Stone Marshes

Temple Farm

Littlebrook
Farm

Cotton
Farm

Greenhithe

Ingress Abbey

Priory
Works

104

RAILWAY

STONE

Station

20

Dartfordcreek
Paper Mill

Branch

St Mary

St Mary's

50

Ga

Phœnix
Mill

100

50

Horns Cross

115

Knockholt
Farm

Eastern

Barnesfield

North

Kent

Lunatic
Asylum

Stonelodge
Farm

Stone
Castle

Alkerden
Farm

DARTFORD

126

T.P.

Woodlands

186

Cemetery

Mounts
Wood

Swa

118

171

191

Cranford
Lodge

134

Hungrygut Hall

224

100

Grangetree
Farm

Dartford
Powder Mills

The Downs

200

Stonewood

200

50

100

Bean

235

Gore

39

100

Hollands

100

Darenth

300

Hawley
House

60

Lane End

200

200

Hawley

235

Wood

Shere Hall

Grange

100

Sutton
Mill

Darenth

99

St Margaret's

Sutton
Place

67

Green Street
Green

Clement
Street

St John's

Westwood
Farm

100

St Margarets

163

St John's

Martin's
Farm

12

Sutton
at Hone

Walnuttree
Farm

Gildenhill F.

South
Darenth

Gill's Farm

Farningham
Road Statⁿ

Pinden

Chatham

and

Dover

RAILWAY

200

106

200

1   2

1 mile approx.

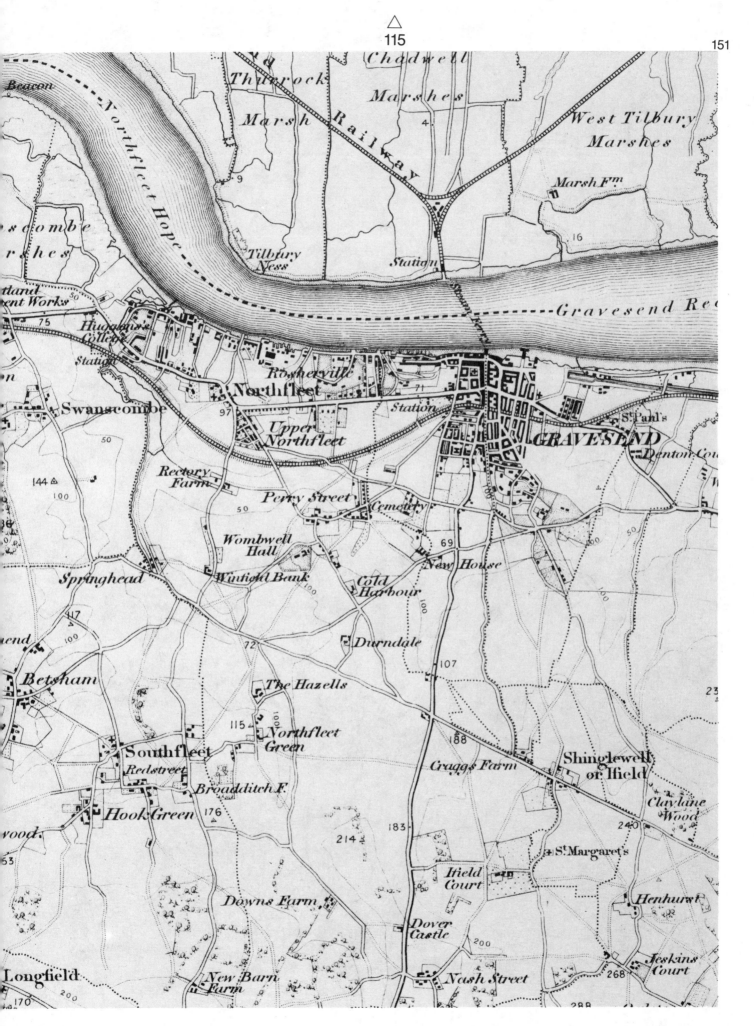

Chadwell
Marshes
Thurrock
Marsh
West Tilbury
Marshes
Railway
4
Marsh F^m
Beacon
Northfleet Hope
9
16
Tilbury
Ness
Station
scombe
rshes
Gravesend Rea
land
ent Works
50
75
Huggens
College
Rosherville
Station
Northfleet
71
GRAVESEND
Swanscombe
97
Station
St Paul's
50
Upper
Northfleet
Denton Cou
W
Rectory
Farm
Perry Street
Cemetery
144 △
100
50
69
New House
Wombwell
Hall
Cold
Harbour
50
Springhead
Winfield Bank
100
100
117
100
72
Durndale
100
107
Betsham
The Hazells
188
23
115
100
Northfleet
Green
Southfleet
Craggs Farm
Shinglewell
or Ifield
Redstreet
Claylane
Wood
Broadditch F.
176
240
Hook Green
St Margaret's
214
183
Ifield
Court
Henhurst
wood
Downs Farm
53
Dover
Castle
200
Jeskins
Court
Longfield
268
New Barn
Farm
Nash Street
170
200
288

Surveyed 1866-1868. Published 1876

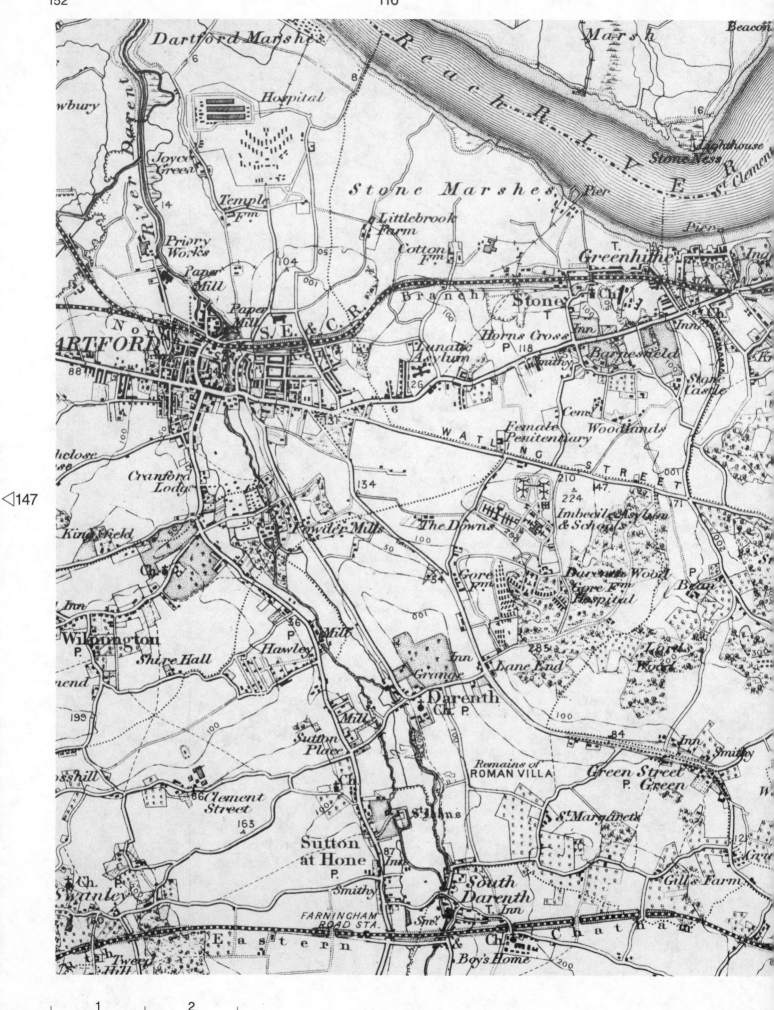

116

◁147

1   2

1 mile approx.

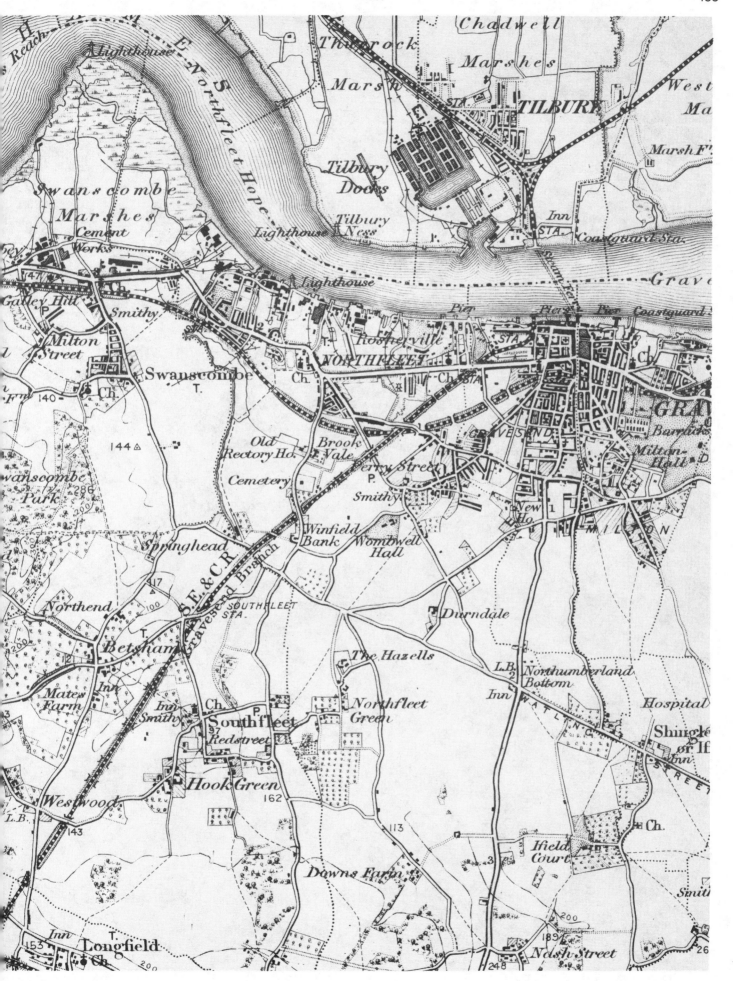

Surveyed 1861-1868. Revised 1903. Published 1905.

124

1 mile approx.

Published 1816.

△ 126

1 mile approx.

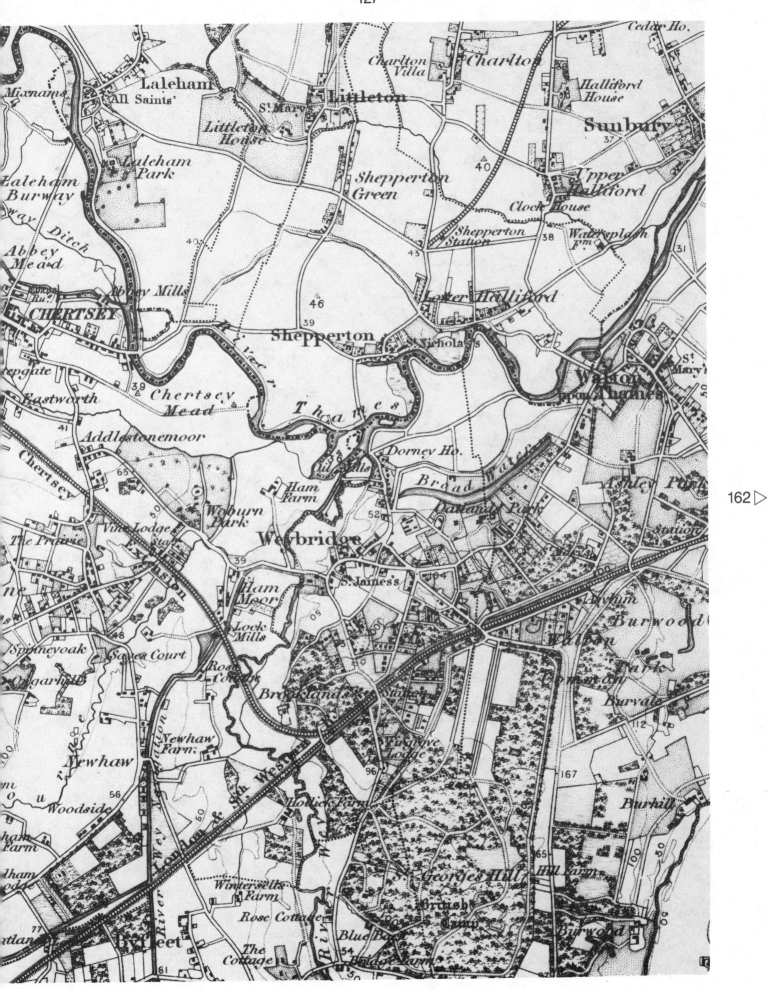

Surveyed 1874. Published 1880.

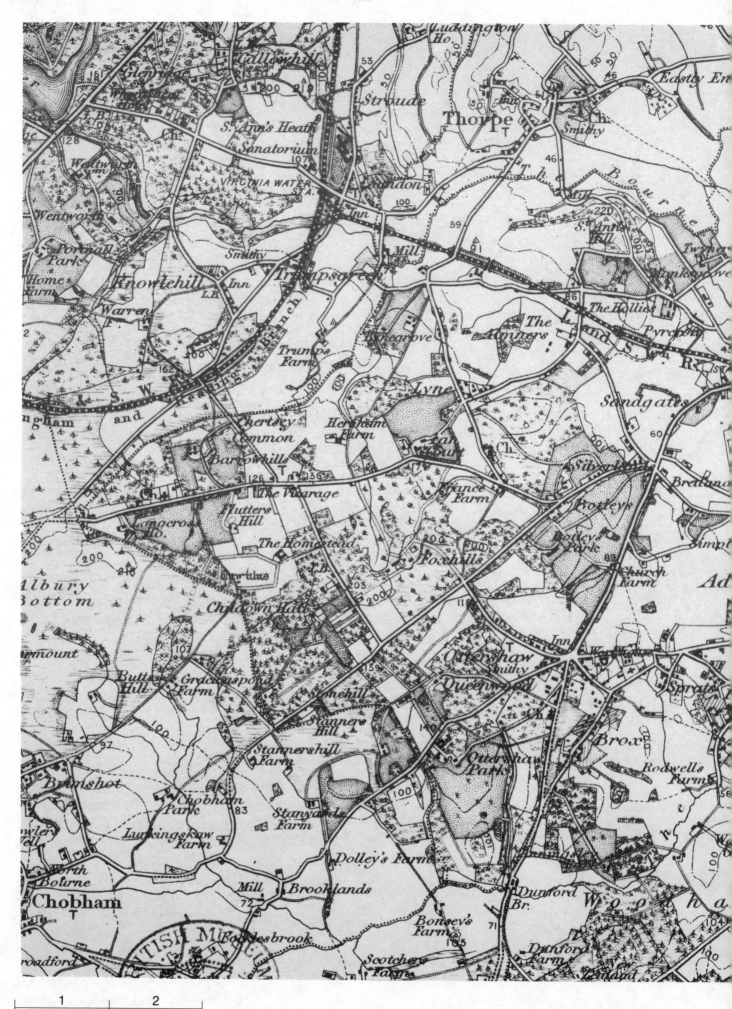

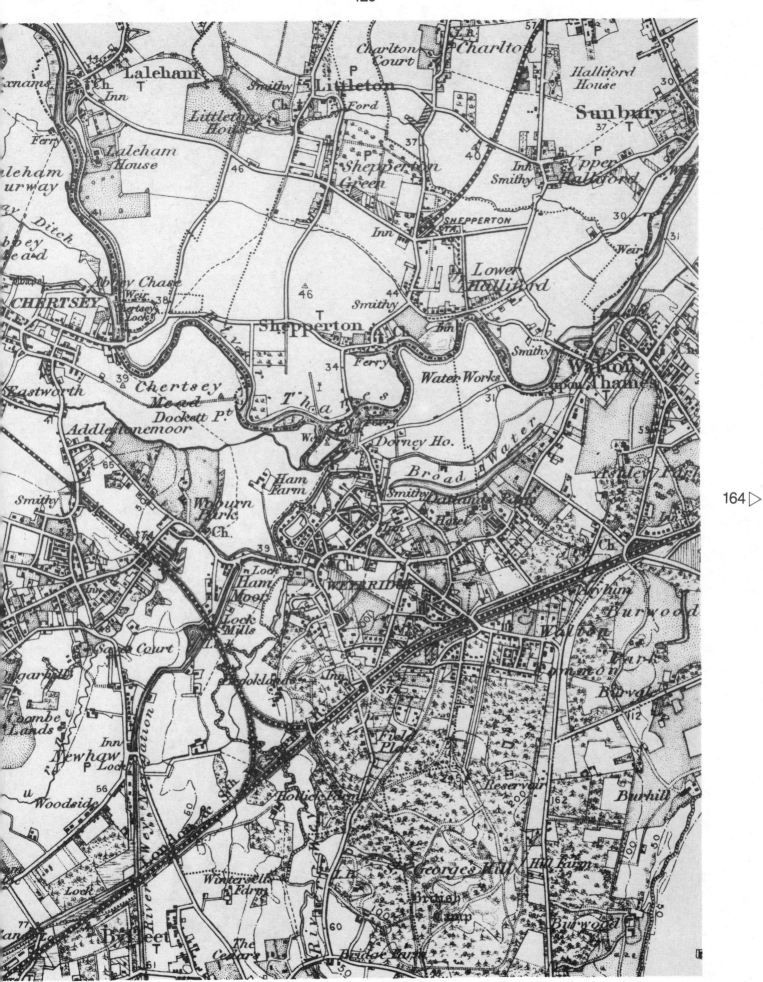

164 ▷

Surveyed 1863-1874. Revised 1901-1902. Published 1904.

West Moulsey

Hampton Court Br.

East Moulsey

Apps Court

Dunstable Common

E. Moulsey Com.

Thame Ditton

Parsonage

Ember Court

Walton on Thames

Walton Park

Stock F.

Weston Green

Walton Vale Cottage

Ditton Marsh

Iron Mills

Esher Place

Sanddown F.

T. Pits

Cottage

Hersham

River Mole

Esher

Broad Lane

Hare Lane

Green

urwood

Westend

Abourne

Claremont Park

Bushill

Southwood

inter Down

Fair-Mile

Esher Com.

Stoke Heath F.

urwood Ho.

Cobham Com.

Marsh Place

Old Com.

Fair Mile F.

Common

Stoke Lane

Jessops Well

Warren

Stoke

Heady

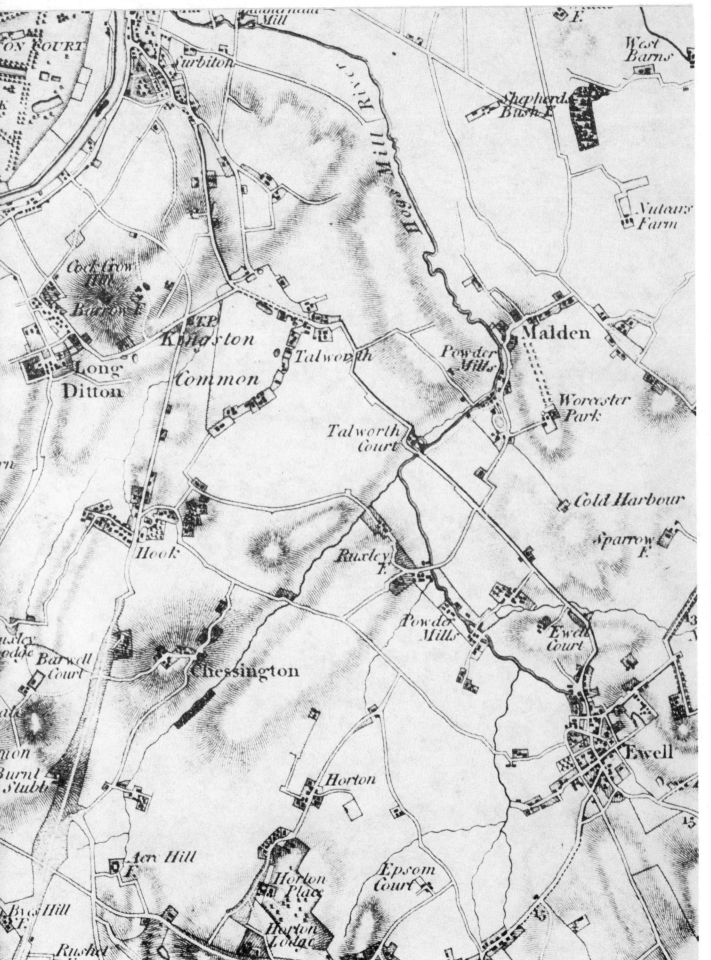

Published 1819.

◁157

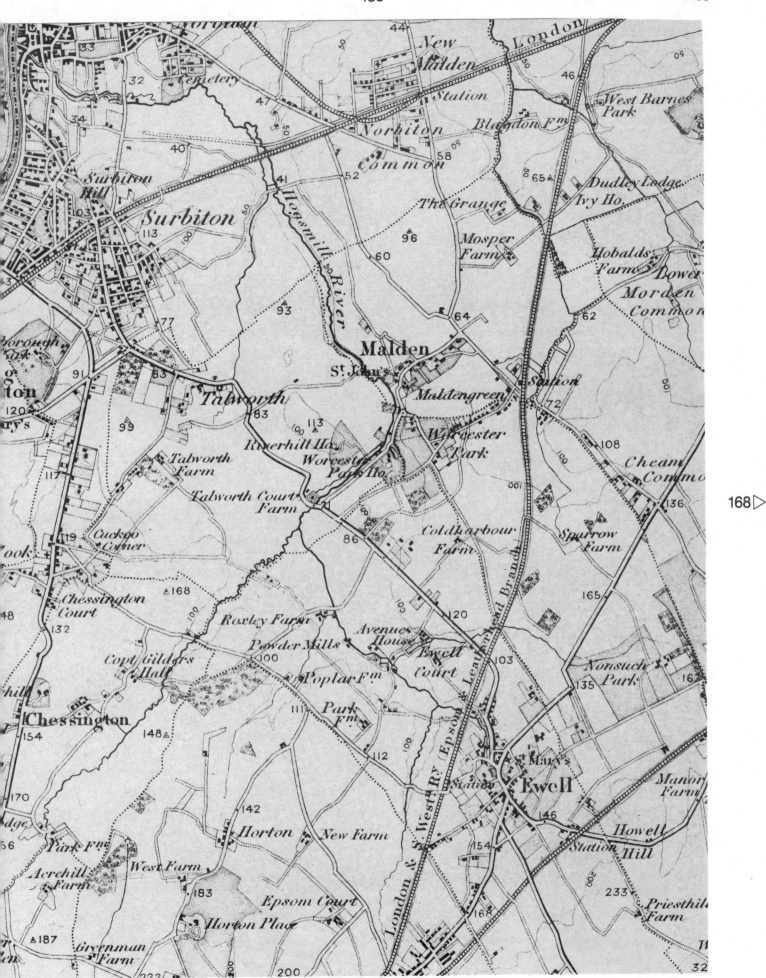

168 ▷

Surveyed 1861-1868. Published 1876.

◁159

1

2

1 mile approx.

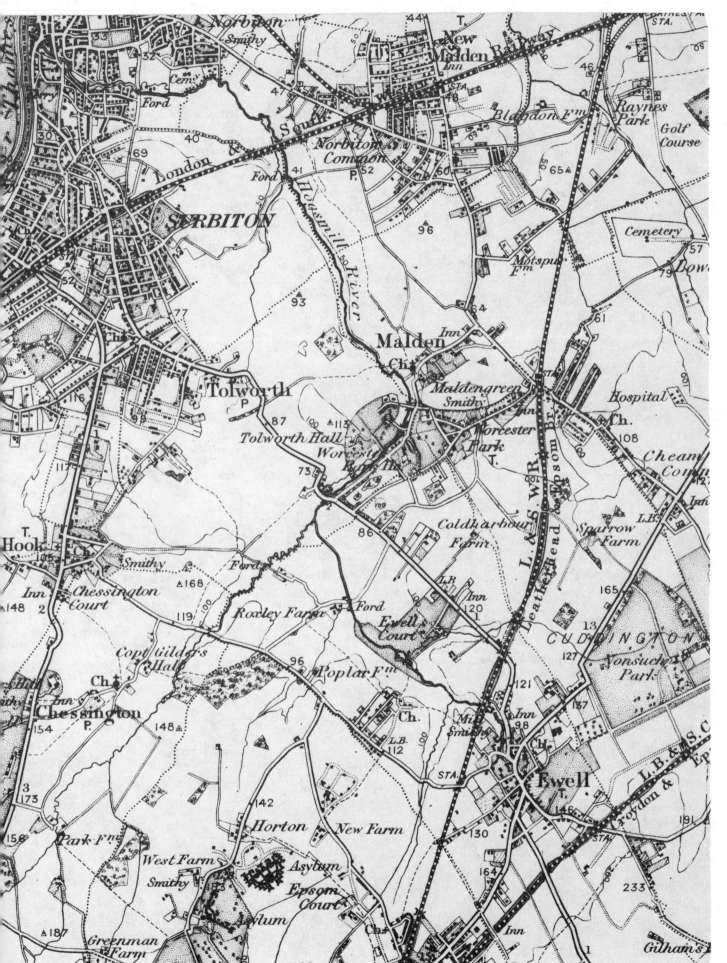

Norbiton
Smithy
Cemy
Ford
New Malden Railway
Inn
STA.
Blagdon Fm
Raynes Park
Golf Course
London South
Norbiton Common
P.
SURBITON
Hogsmill River
Ford
96
Cemetery
Motspur Fm
Dow
93
Malden
Inn
Ch.
Maldengreen
Smithy
Hospital
Th.
Tolworth
P.
Worcester Park
Inn
Ch eam Com
Tolworth Hall
Worcester Park Fm
Coldharbour Farm
L.&.S.W.R.
Sparrow Farm
Leatherhead & Epsom Br.
Hook
T.
Smithy
Ford
Ewell Court
L.B.
Inn
CUDDINGTON
Chessington Court
Inn
Roxley Farm
Ford
Nonsuch Park
Copt Gilders Hall
Poplar Fm
Ch.
Mill
Smithy
Inn
Ch.
Ewell
Chessington
P.
L.B.
STA.
L.B. &.S.C.
Horton
New Farm
Croydon & Ep
STA.
Park Fm
West Farm
Smithy
Asylum
Epsom Court
Inn
Gilham's
Greenman Farm
Asylum
Ch.

Surveyed 1861-1868. Revised 1903. Published 1905.

Morton
Common

Mitcham

Cannon
Hill

Mordon
Park

9

Snuff
Mill

Mitcham
Grove

Mill

Work H

Mitc
Com

Lower
Mordon

10

Iron

Mordon

T.F.

Pig F.
Stone Cot
Hill

10

Callico
Grounds

Beddington
Corner

Bedd
P

Park
F.

Pyford
Bridge

Mill
Mill Way

◁161

12

Sutton
Grove

Brick
Yard

Hackbridge

Work
Ho.

Rye

Oil
Mill

Mill

Been
Hill

Carshalton

Walling

12

Sutton

Cheam

Little
Cheam

Carshalton
Park

nesuch
Park

13

B   A   N   S   T   E   A   D

Barn

Barrow
Hedges

gn

Howell
Hill

Cottage

13

Sutton
Lodge

D   O   W   N   S

Here
Warren

Barn

Hundred
Acres

Hungry
Bottom

Cornhill

1   2

1 mile approx.

Gilpens F.

Leatha Bottom

Fernham Wood

Parchmoor

Whitehouse Wood

Goat Ho.

Blind Corner

Clay Lane

Beech

Colliars Water

White Ho. F.

Sellhurst

9 Acre Wood

Thornton Heath
9

Sellhurst Wood

Woodside

18 Acre Wood

6

Way

Broad Green
7

Croydon Common

Common Place

Addiscombe House

Shirley

10

Barracks

Bleaching

Flour M.

Snuff M.

Waddon Flour

Waddon

Dubber Hill

CROYDON

Park Hill

Combe F.

Combe House

Sand

Cold Harbour

Havling House

Combe Lane

Greng F.

Ballards

9

Combe Hill

Beggars Bush

Woodcote

Bottom

Purley F.

Purley Ho.

Selsdon

Selsdon

T.P.

Sanderstead

Published 1819.

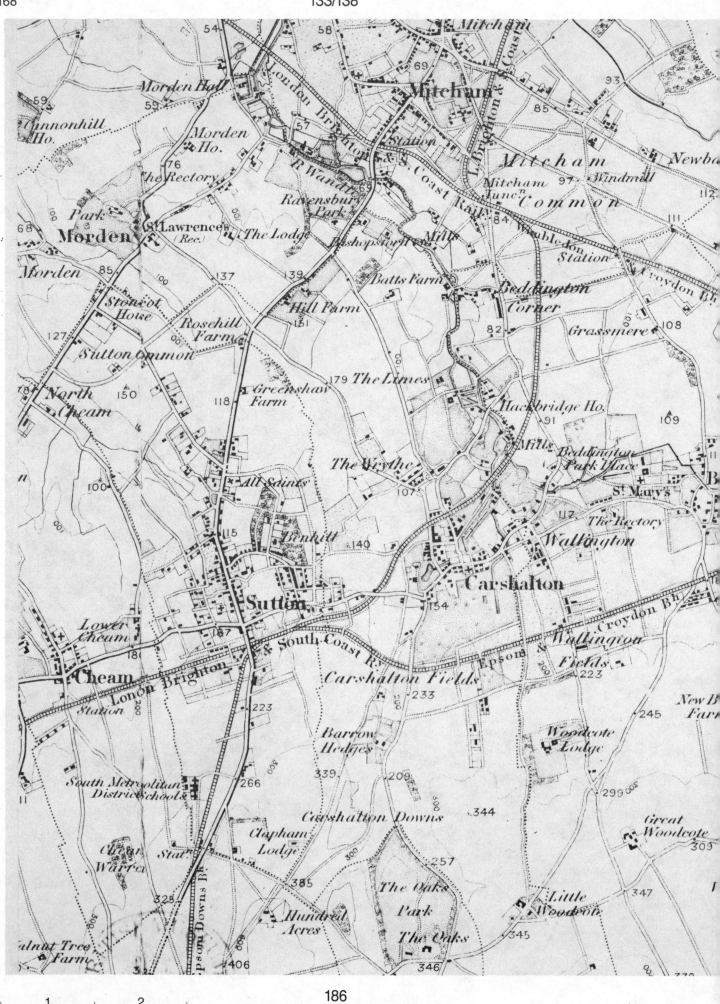

◁ 163

1   2

1 mile approx.

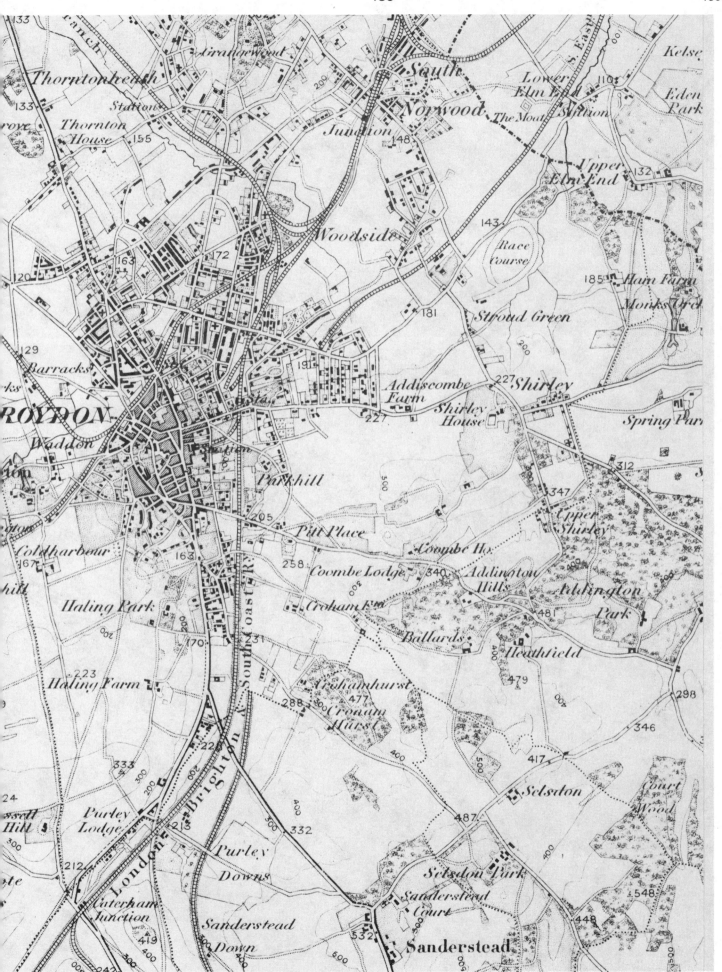

Surveyed 1861-1868. Published 1876.

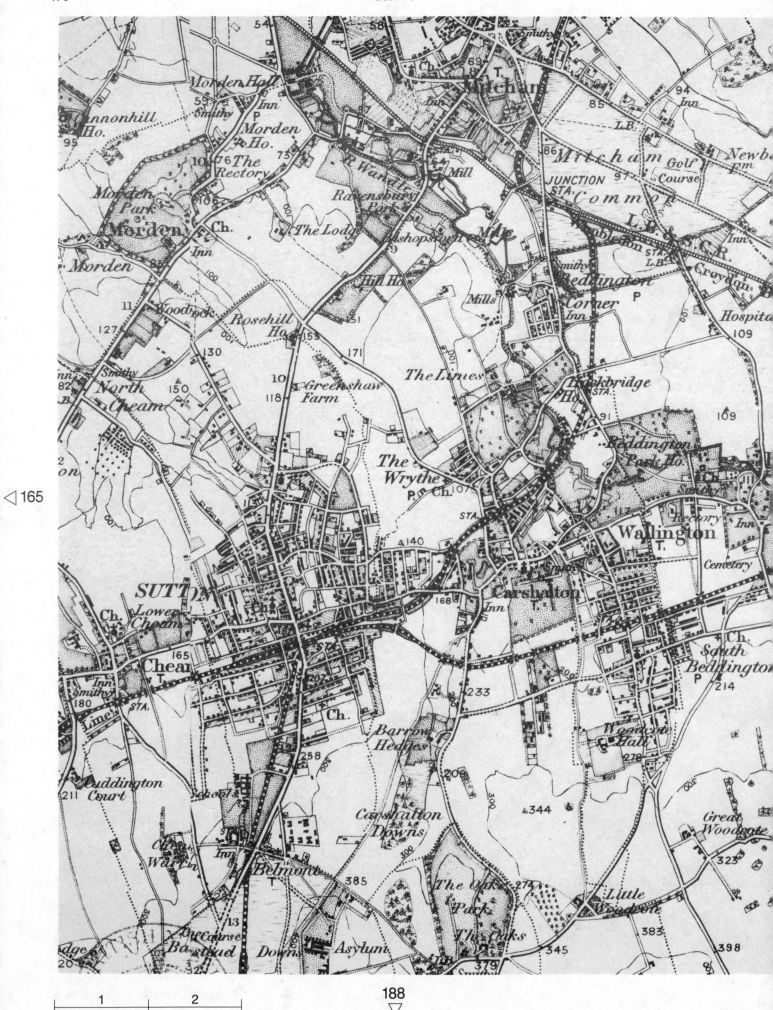

1   2

1 mile approx.

Surveyed 1861-1868. Revised 1903. Published 1905.

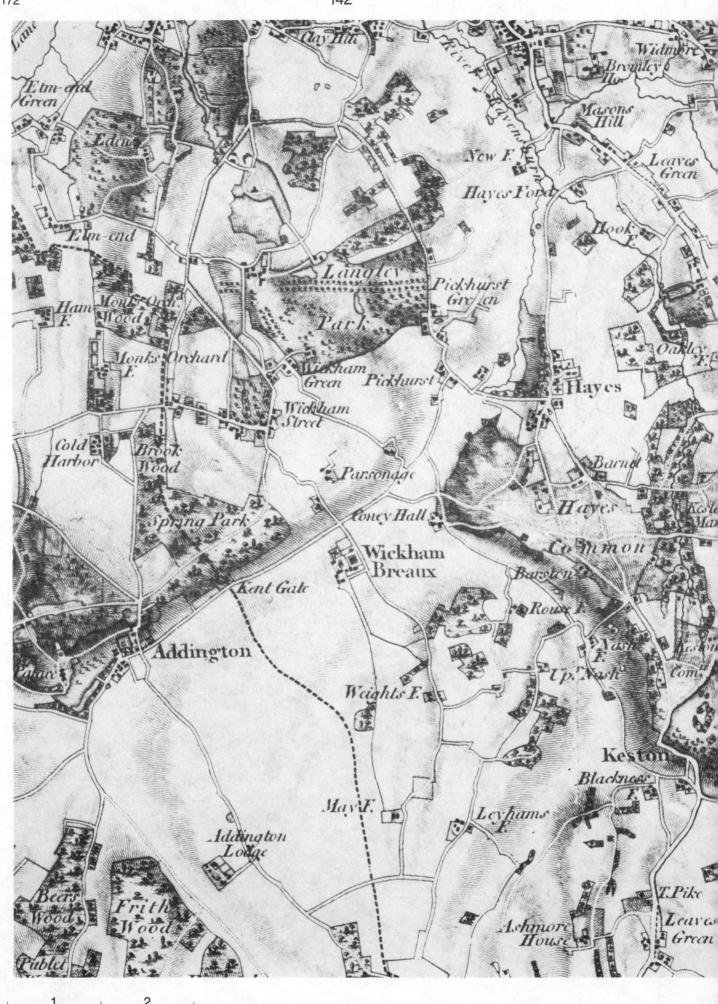

△

◁167

Clay Hill

River Ravensbourne

Widmore

Bromley H.

Masons Hill

New F.

Leaves Green

Hayes Ford

Hook F.

Elm-end Green

Eden

Langley

Pickhurst Green

Elm-end

Ham F.

Monks Orch. Wood

Park

Wickham Green

Pickhurst

Hayes

Monks Orchard F.

Wickham Street

Oakley F.

Cold Harbor

Brook Wood

Parsonage

Barnet

Hayes

Spring Park

Coney Hall

Common

Kent Gate

Wickham Breaux

Barston

Roux F.

Addington

Up.ʳ Nash

Keston Com.

Palace

Weights F.

Keston

Blacknes F.

May F.

Leyhams F.

Addington Lodge

Beers Wood

Frith Wood

Ashmore House

T. Pike

Leaves Green

Publet

St Pauls
Cray

St Pauls
Hill

St Pauls
Cray Comⁿ

St Marys
Cray

Kevin

Hawker
Wood

Povetch

Mill

Place

Southborough

Mill

Cockmalling F.

Town
Court

Crofton
Court

Broom
Hill

Petting
Grove

Magpie
Hall

Crofton

Orpington

Woods

Tripe
F.

Crofton Pound

Crofton

Uppington
F.

Gorrington
F.

Brestes
Green

Locks
Bottom

Tate
Wood

Wellbrook
Wood

Chelshel

Farnboro
Hall

Bushey
Coppia

Farnborough

Greenstreet
Green

Pax F

High-elms
F.

Worlds End

North
End

Farthing Street

New Hol

T.Pike

Broke
F.

Orange Court

Gorrings
F.

Stonerock

Spratts
Bottom

Down

Norsted

Hals

Published 1819.

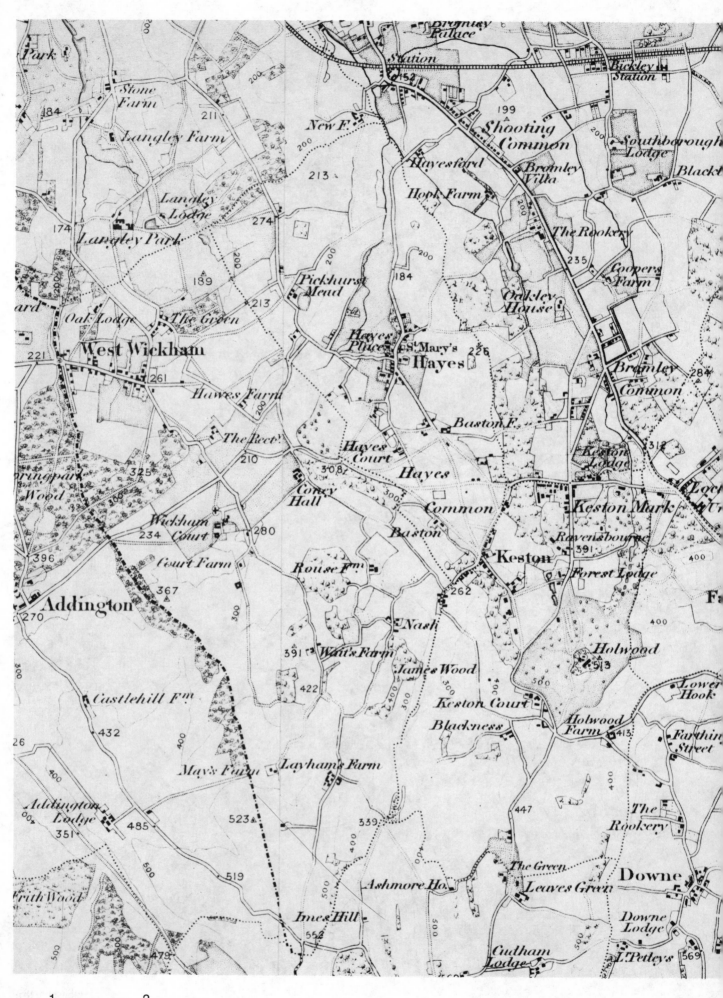

◁169

1 mile approx.

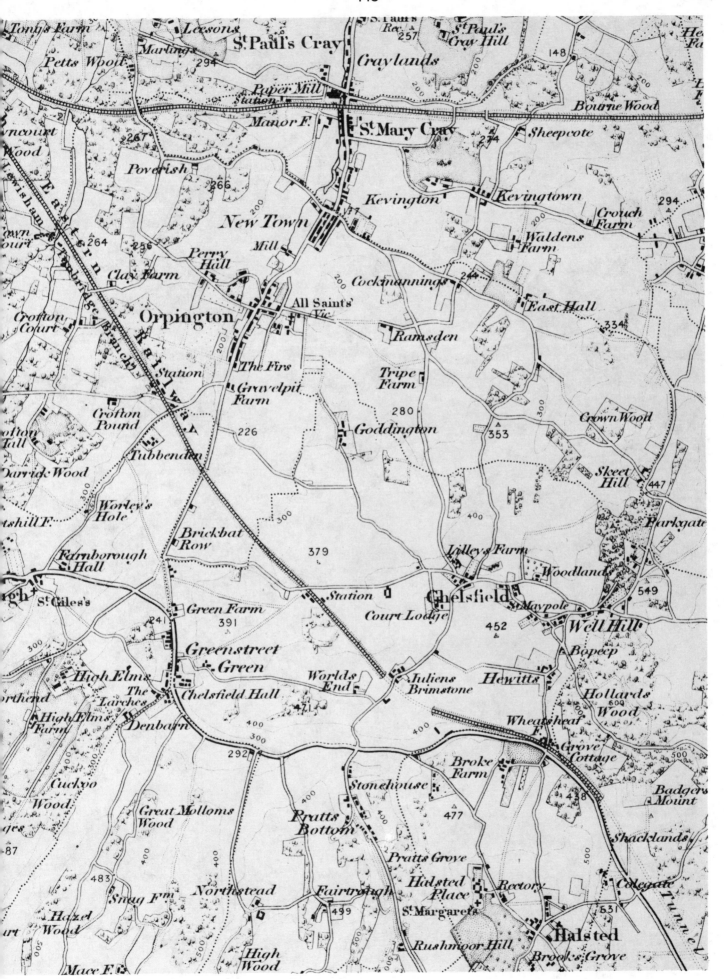

Surveyed 1861-1868. Published 1876.

◁171

1   2

1 mile approx.

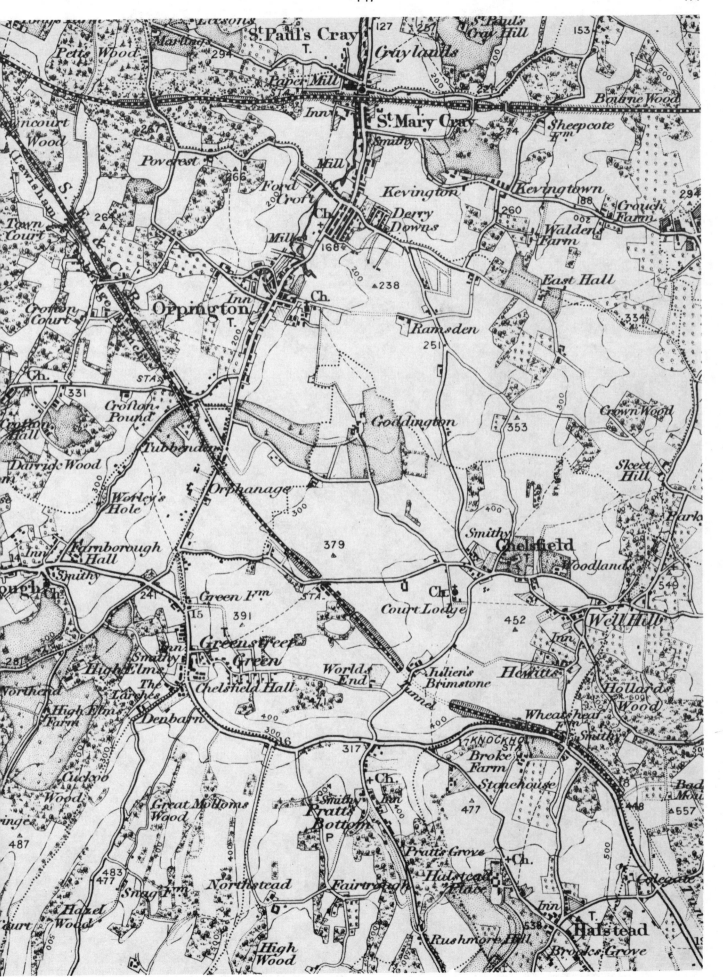

Surveyed 1861-1871. Revised 1901-2. Published 1904.

Cobham Street

Brooks Place

Green

Little Heath

Ockshot Street

Cobham

Cobham Tilt

Cobham Park

Leatherhead Common

Bullocks F.

Downside

Down Mill

Stoke D'Abernon

Well Ho.

Slyfield F.

Platsome Green

Sheep Bell F.

Randall Ho.

Fetcham Common

Farm

Isle of Wight

Mill

Bookham Common

The Rough

Effingham

Com.

Fetcham

Barn

Eastwick Park

Fe tc ham

Ire Wood

Little Bookham

Great Bookham

Barn

Effingham

Rorring Ho.

Downs

Common

Fields

Phenia F.

Published 1816

△

Stoke Wood

122

Telegraph
Hill

Brewery

Kniphill Farm   155   246   Oak Shade

Leighill Farm   100   Little
Heath

Church Cobham   Oxshott   Newpond Ho

St Andrew's   Knowlehill   Charlwood Farm   Pachesham
Park

Brook Farm   118   83

Cobham
Till   97   Stoke Lodge   Leatherhead Common

Cobham Park   Stoke   130   Woodlands   Oak Lawn
D'Abernon   Park

Cobham
Lodge   113   Bowhurst Fm   127

112   St Mary's   Manor Ho.   Brickfield

Downside   Sawmill   Pachesham

Downside Farm   90   100

153   Slyfield House   172

9   New Barn Farm   Millfield   Bar

141   Bookham
Lodge   Sheepbell Fm   Randalls Park   Randalls   129
Farm   Gas
T.P.

Dudwick Farm   Brytnes Fm   Barracks Farm   167   Cannoncourt   Station
116   219   Farm

Newmarsh   100   200   Monksgreen   Fetcham Mill
Farm   Farm

116   Great Bookham   127
Common   Fetcham Lodge

Banks   Little   Fetcham
Common   Bookham   Thorncroft
116   Common   153

Norwood Farm   Church   Fetcham
Park   200

Petty's Farm   Lonesome   The Kennels   Park Farm
Farm

Lower Farm   155   223   294   Bocketts Farm
154   Eastwick Park   Eastwick   Give
Gro

Indian   St Nicholas
Farm   200   Great Bookham

189   Little   Roaringhouse Farm
200   Bookham   The Grange   285   Fetcham   The Prior
Down s   464
Church   The Rectory   Norbury Park

Orestan Farm   St Lawrence's   286   Common Fields
239

Effingham   292

The Villa   Effingham Ho.   354   Goldstone Farm   Lodge Farm

Phœnix Farm
466

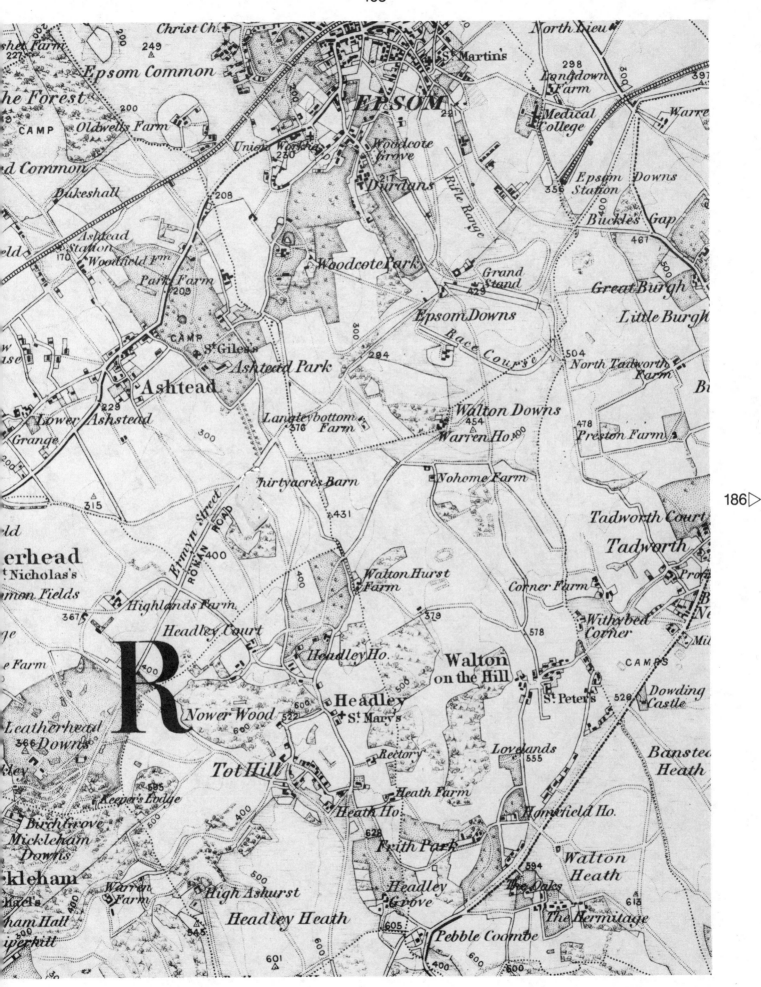

Surveyed 1866-1871. Published 1878.

△
164

▽

1   2

1 mile approx.

188▷

Surveyed 1866-1871. Revised 1901. Published 1904.

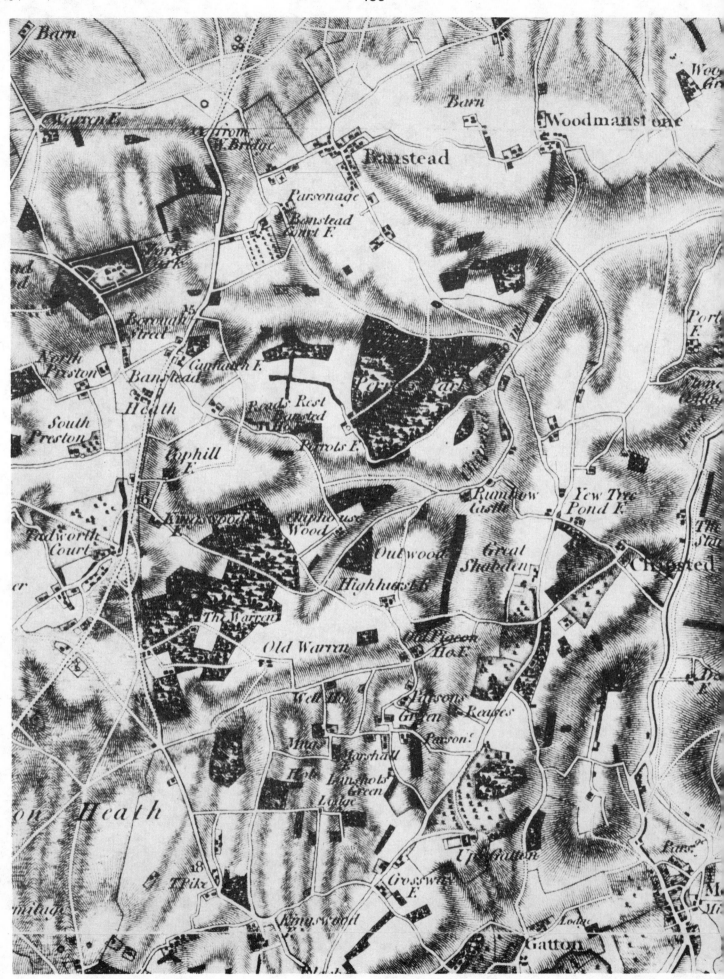

◁179

1

2

1 mile approx.

Published 1816.

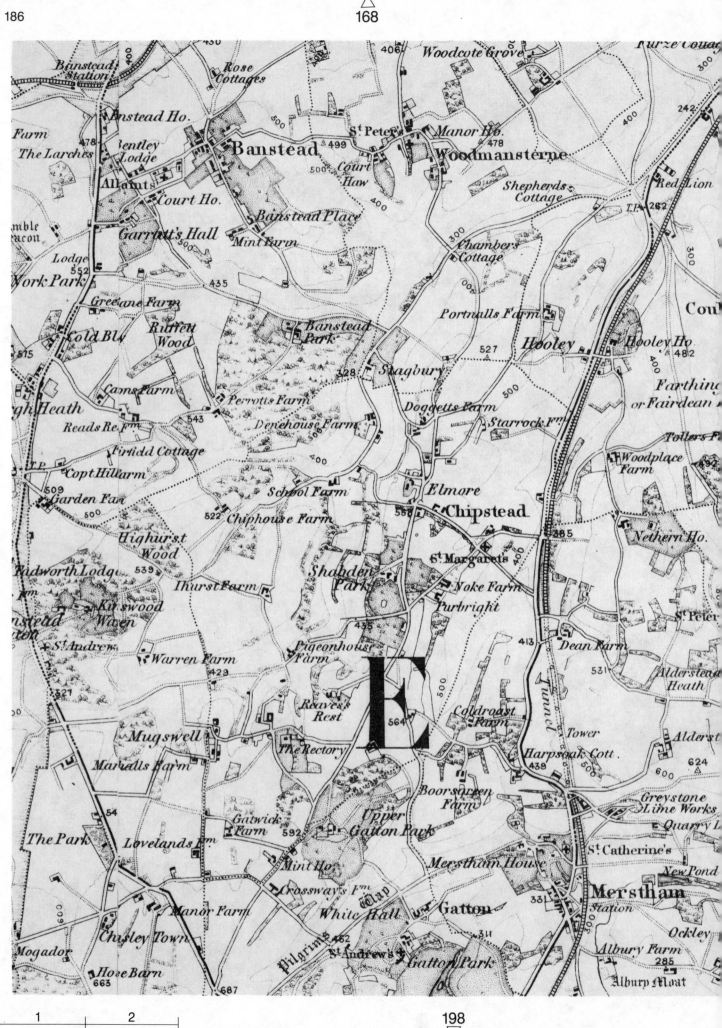

Banstead Station

400

430

Rose Cottages

Woodcote Grove

406

Furze Cottage

300

Farm

The Larches

478

Bentley Lodge

Enstead Ho.

Banstead

499

St Peter

Manor Ho.

478

Woodmansterne

400

242

Red Lion

300

Allsaints

Court Ho.

500

Court Haw

Shepherds Cottage

400

T.P. 282

Garratt's Hall

Banstead Place

Mint Farm

300

Chambers Cottage

York Park

Lodge

552

435

400

527

Portnalls Farm

Hooley

500

Hooley Ho.

482

Cou

Greeane Farm

Ruffett Wood

Banstead Park

Stagbury

Doggetts Farm

Starrock Fm.

Farthing or Fairdean

Cold Bl

Cams Farm

328

Perrotts Farm

Denehouse Farm

Tollers F

515

gh Heath

Reads Re. Fm.

543

500

Woodplace Farm

892

T.P

Firtidd Cottage

Copt Hill Farm

509

400

School Farm

558

Elmore

Chipstead

Nethern Ho.

Garden Fm

Highurst Wood

500

522

Chiphouse Farm

285

St Margarets

400

adworth Lodge

539

Thurst Farm

Shabden Park

Noke Farm

St Peter

Kiswood Waren

435

Purbright

413

Dean Farm

531

nstead tion

St Andrew

Warren Farm

Pigeonhouse Farm

500

Aldersteads Heath

527

429

E

564

Coldroast Farm

Tunnel

Tower

Alderst

Mugswell

Reaves Rest

Harpsoak Cott.

439

624

Marralls Farm

The Rectory

600

Greystone Lime Works

54

Gatwick Farm

592

Upper Gatton Park

Boorsoreen Farm

300

St Catherine's

Quarry L

The Park

Lovelands Fm.

Mint Ho.

Merstham House

New Pond

Manor Farm

Crossways Fm.

White Hall

Gatton

331

Merstham Station

Ockley

600

Chasley Town

462

Pilgrim

311

Albury Farm

285

Mogador

Hose Barn

663

687

St Andrews

Gatton Park

Albury Moat

1   2

1 mile approx.

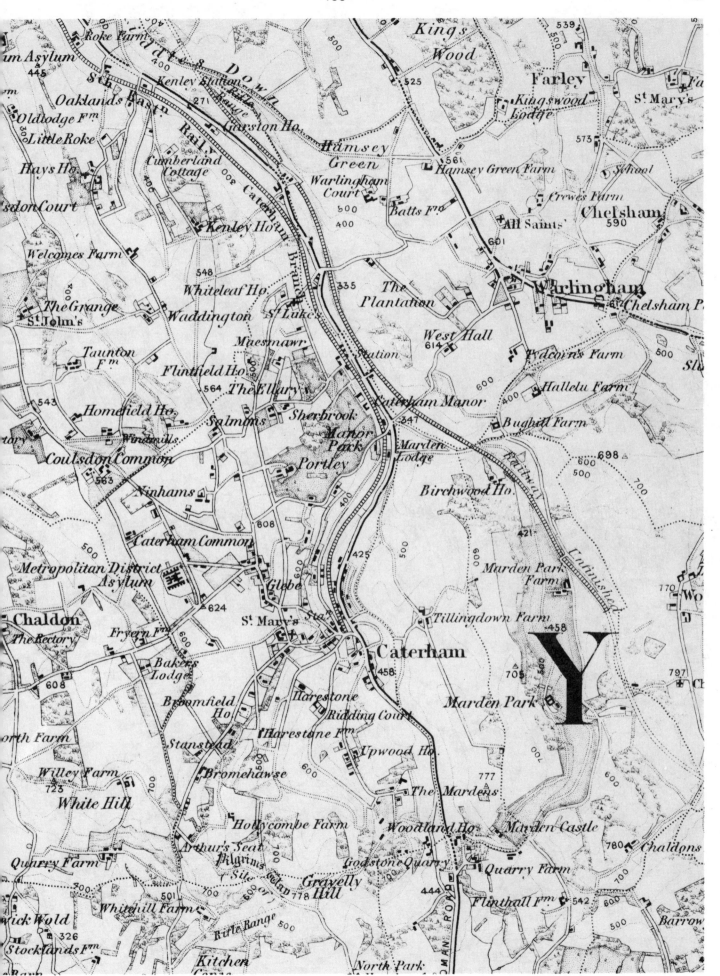

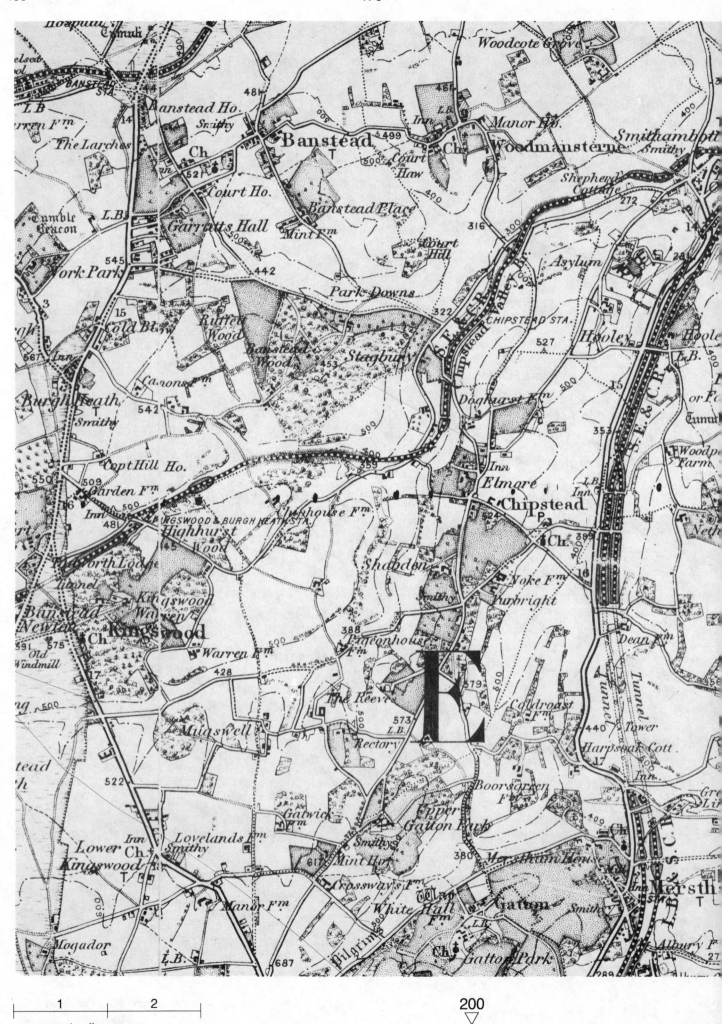

183

1   2

1 mile approx.

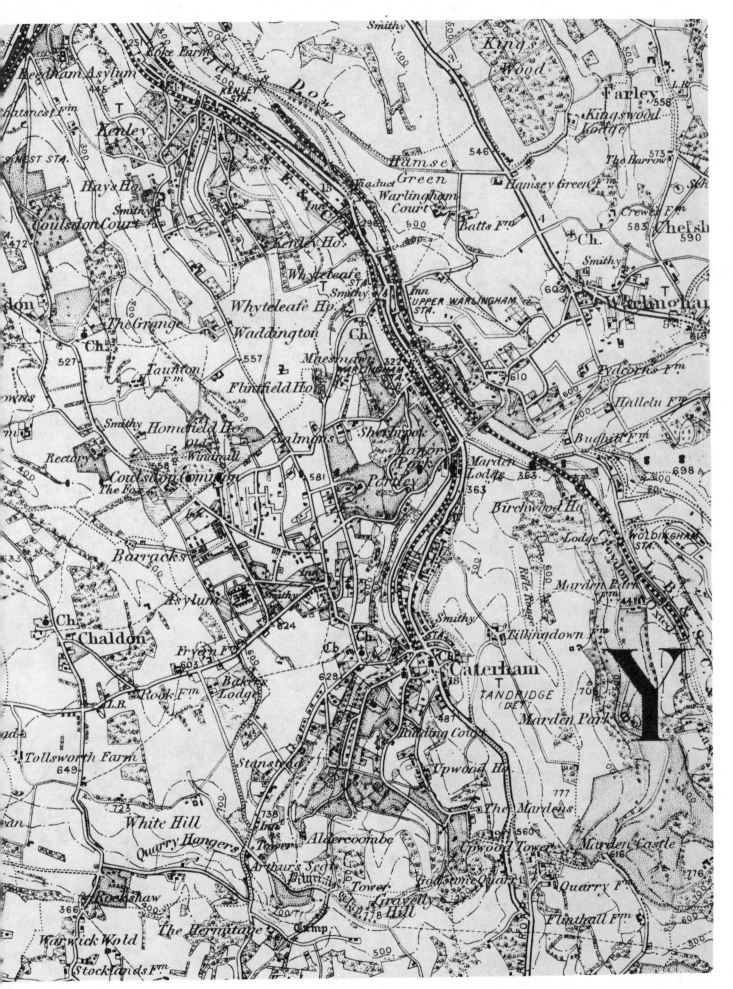

Surveyed 1866-1871. Revised 1901. Published 1904.

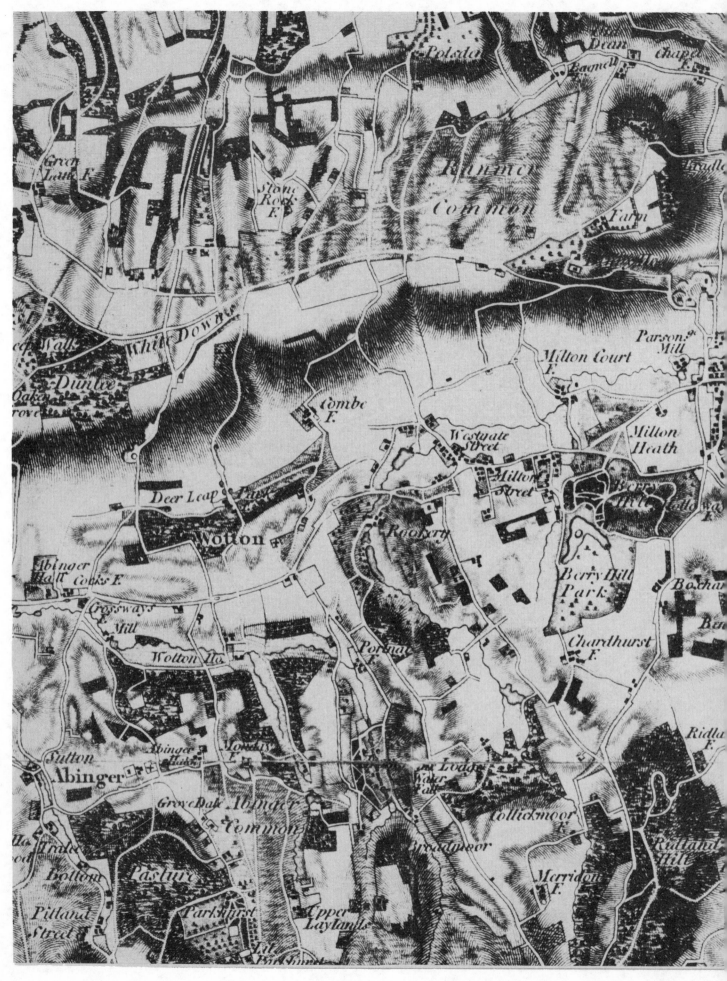

178

196 ▷

Hopps

Parsonage

Hill F.

Buc
Green

Tranquil
Dale

Buckland

Moor Place

Worum Ho

Mill
Tranquil
Hill

Bare
Mill

Box Hill

Betchworth
Castle

Betchworth

Punch
Bowl

Mill

DORKING

Brockham
Green

Snower
Hill

Park F.

Providence

Rice
Br.

Chart

Gadbrook
Com.n

Park

Parkpale
F.

Leigh Place

Glory

Stove Br.

Stubs
F.

Scammel
F.

Farnells
Com.n

Dawes
Green

Leigh

Dun
Common

Leigh
Br.

Stumblehole
F.

Brockham
Common

Nultewood
Common

Shelwood
Com.n

Holmwood

Shelwood F.

Hill Ho

Common

Hernbead
F.

Peters F.

Ewood
F.

Ewood

Published 1816.

△
180

1 mile approx.

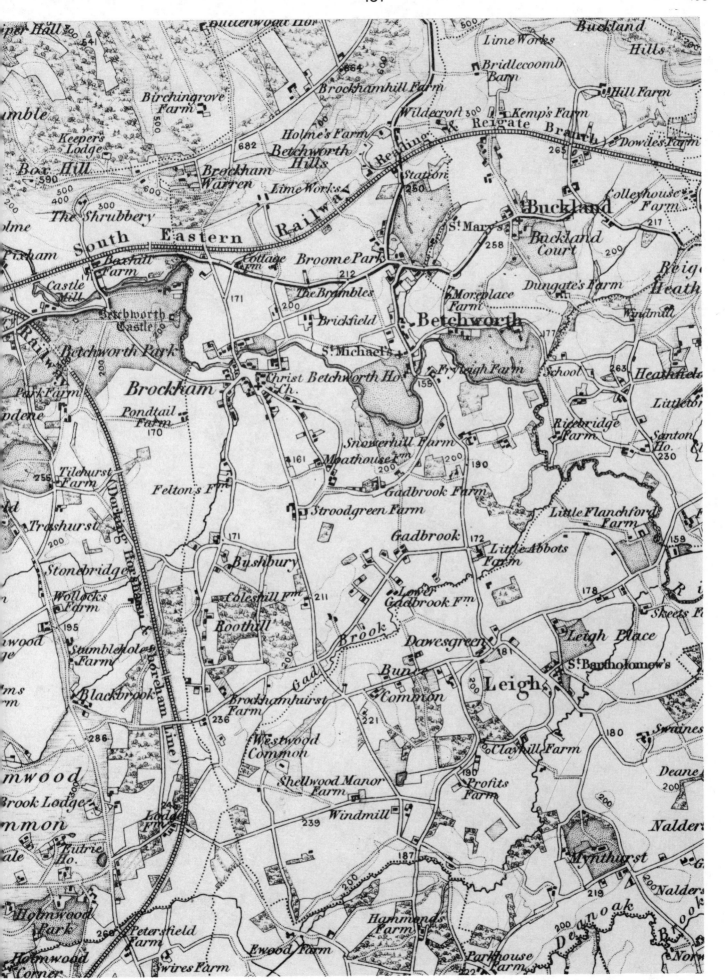

Surveyed 1866-1871. Published 1878.

△
182

1 mile approx.

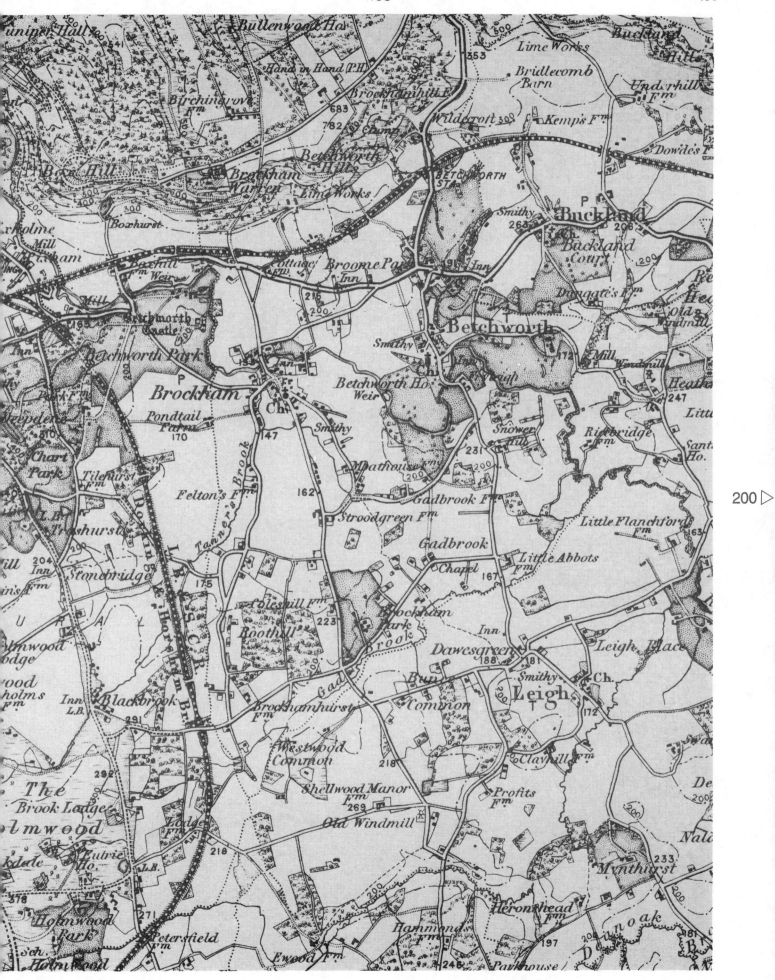

200 ▷

Surveyed 1866-71. Revised 1901. Published 1904.

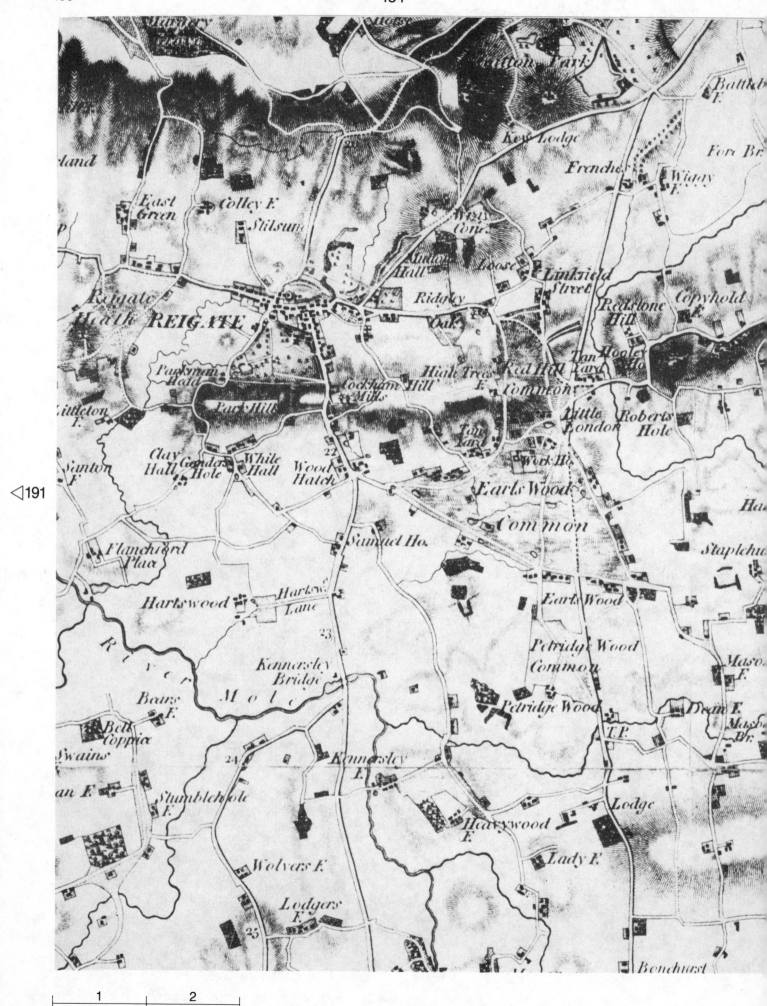

△
184

◁191

East
Green

Colley F.

Stilsunt

Reigate
Heath   REIGATE

Parkman
Head

Park Hill

Littleton
F.

Clay
Hall

Gender
Hole

While
Hall

Wood
Hatch

22

Santon
F.

Flanchford
Place

Hartswood

Hartsw
Lane

23

River

Mole

Kennersley
Bridge

Bears
F.

Bell
Coppice

Swains

an F.

24

Stumblehole
F.

Kennersley
F.

Wolvers F.

Lodgers
F.

25

Catton Park

Kew Lodge

Frenches

Battleb
F.

Fore Br.

Wiggy
F.

Wiggy
Corn.

Mudot
Hall

Loose

Ridgley

Oak

Linkfield
Street

Redstone
Hill

Copyhold

Hooley
Ho.

Tan Yard

High Trees
F.

Red Hill
Common

Cockham
Mills

Tan
Yard

Little
London

Roberts
Hole

Work Ho.

Earls Wood

Common

Ha

Staplehu

Samuel Ho.

Earls Wood

Petridge Wood
Common

Maso
F.

Petridge Wood

Dean F.

Mash
Br.

T.P.

Lodge

Heavywood
F.

Lady F.

Benchurst

Published 1816.

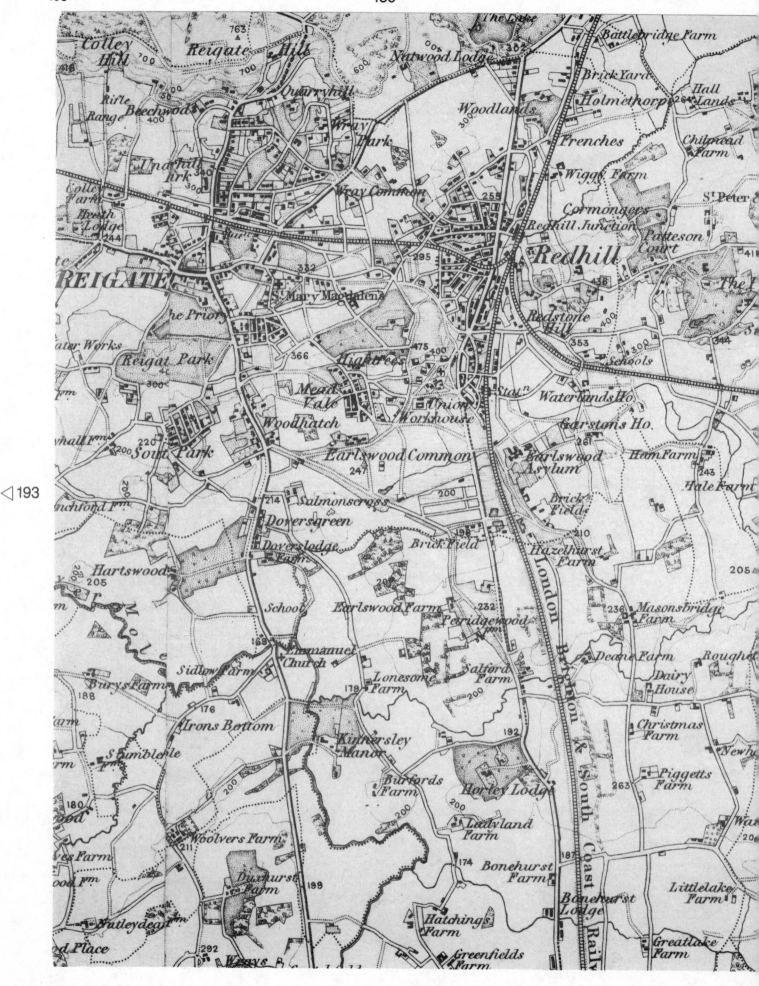

△ 193

Colley Hill

Reigate Hill

763

700

700

Rifle Range

Beechwood

400

500

Una Hill Park

340

300

Colley Farm

Heath Lodge

244

REIGATE

The Priory

Water Works

Reigate Park

40

300

332

St Mary Magdalene

Quarryhill

Wray Park

Wray Common

Nutwood Lodge

400

600

600

300

258

295

The Lake

Battlebridge Farm

Brick Yard

Holmethorpe

Woodlands

Frenches

Wigg Farm

Cormongers

Redhill Junction

Redhill

264

Hall Lands

Chilmead Farm

St Peter

Patteson Court

41

The

366

Highfrees

Mead Vale

475 400

Redstone Hill

353

400

300

342

Schools

Farm

Woodhatch

Union Workhouse

Sta n

Waterlands Ho

Garstons Ho.

200

South Park

220

Earlswood Common

247

Earlswood Asylum

Ham Farm

261

243

Hale Farm

214

Salmonscross

Doversgreen

200

Brick Fields

Hartswood

205

Doverslodge Farm

School

Earlswood Farm

Brick Field

196

210

Hazelhurst Farm

205

169

Emmanuel Church

232

Perridgewood m

236

Masonsbridge Farm

Sidlow Farm

Burys Farm

188

Lonesome Farm

179

Salford Farm

200

Deane Farm

Dairy House

Roughet

176

Irons Bottom

192

Christmas Farm

Newl

Stumblehole

Kinnersley Manor

Burfords Farm

200

200

Horley Lodge

263

Piggetts Farm

180

Woolvers Farm

211

200

Ladyland Farm

174

Bonehurst Farm

187

Bonehurst Lodge

Littlelake Farm

Wa

20

292

Duxhurst Farm

189

Hatchings Farm

Nutleydean Fm

d Place

Greatlake Farm

Ways

Greenfields Farm

1

2

1 mile approx.

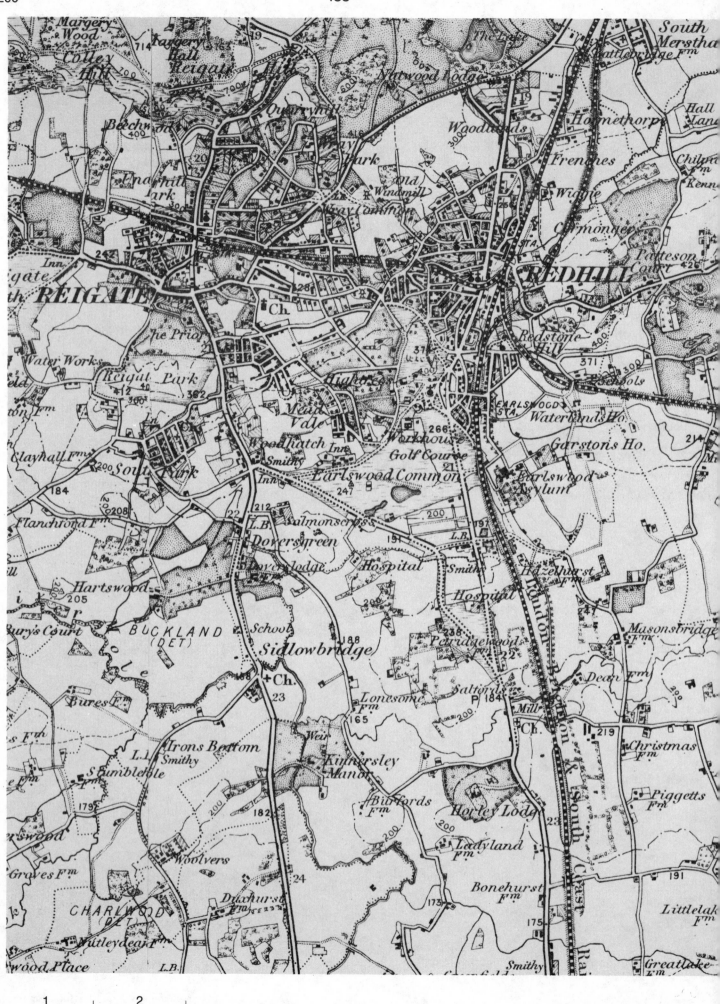

◁195

1 mile approx.

Surveyed 1866-71. Revised 1901. Published 1904.

BIBLIOGRAPHY

Greater London: Edited by J.T. Coppock & Hugh C. Price. Published by Faber & Faber Ltd.

London Recollected: Walter Thornbury & Edward Walford. Published by The Alderman Press

The Historian's Guide to Ordnance Survey Maps: J.B. Harley B.A., PH.D. Published by The National Council of Social Service.

Victoria's London – The Suburbs: Percy Fitzgerald. Published by The Alderman Press.

Village London: Edward Walford. Published by The Alderman Press

Index

Map references are indicated by Roman numerals. e.g. Acton 95 97 99. Places refered to in text by italics e.g. Manor House *6*.